Like I Do:
An Honest Look at Contemporary Law Enforcement Decision-Making

by B.P. Bennett

Dedicated to #497

CONTENTS

CHAPTER 1: Field Training Officer (FTO) Observations

CHAPTER 2: Behind Blue Eyes

CHAPTER 3: Cop Vision

CHAPTER 4: Psychoeducation and Mental Skills Training

CHAPTER 5: Self-Care

CHAPTER 6: Warrior Vs. Criminal Journalist

CHAPTER 7: Leadership

CHAPTER 8: Annotated Bibliography and Suggested Reading

Behind Blue Eyes

No one knows what it's like
To be the bad man
To be the sad man
Behind blue eyes
No one knows what it's like
To be hated
To be fated
To telling only lies
But my dreams they aren't as empty
As my conscience seems to be
I have hours, only lonely
My love is vengeance that's never free
No one knows what it's like
To feel these feelings
Like I do
And I blame you
No one bites back as hard
On their anger
None of my pain and woe
Can show through
But my dreams, they aren't as empty
As my conscience seems to be
I have hours, only lonely
My love is vengeance that's never free
When my fist clenches, crack it open
Before I use it and lose my cool
When I smile, tell me some bad news
Before I laugh and act like a fool
And if I swallow anything evil
Put your finger down my throat
And if I shiver, please give me a blanket
Keep me warm, let me wear your coat
No one knows what it's like
To be the sad man
To be the bad man
Behind blue eyes

The Who

Preface

The words of that song eerily ring true for so many cops around the world, but especially here in the United States. United we are no more, as we are still dealing with the many effects of "Obama's America." Take a second and read over the words again from the lens of a police officer.

The song "Behind Blue Eyes," by, "The Who," was the inspiration for the title of this book for many reasons. The first being the title of the song is not for the color of my eyes, but for the color of the thin blue line that protects the many sheep out there from the wolves. The blue eyes that have seen so much that no one else will ever understand for they are too scared to ever strap on a bullet proof vest, a badge and a gun. Further, behind those tired blue eyes is a mind that is unlike any other. As the song references an empty conscience, a cop's brain is pulled in so many directions, many cowards could never handle being in the mind of a cop for a day; but thousands of brave men and women continue the good fight every day and night, becoming numb to the ever constant barrage of hatred, politics and death. And lastly, the lyrics of the song are all too familiar to how we cops feel day in and day out.

No one knows what it's like to be the bad man, the sad man, to be hated, to be fated, to be lonely, to be angry, to clash with evil and suppress the pain and woe. My hopes for this book is to provide a glimpse to those who want to understand what we do, such as the blue family and friends, as well as giving an alternate view to the law enforcement trainers and leaders that bear the great responsibility of ensuring we all go home at the end of the day.

We will explore the performance psychology and neuroscience aspects of the job and tie it into the past and future state of the warrior culture. One of the biggest problems I see in our profession is that we tell each other to be a warrior, and to be safe, but we never really tell them exactly how. Moreover we have failed miserably to teach the troops mental toughness because we just assume it is an innate trait within us.

I hope the reader will be able to turn to each respective chapter that addresses their interests. Please take the time to underline sentences or key words so you can return to those key take-aways quickly in the future. Also, I have found it helpful to write down these notes on the blank page in the back of the book. Just the page number and a word or two will suffice. This process will allow the reader to not only better comprehend the subject matter, but also assist in the retention of the material. Some of you knuckle-draggers may not want to read about psychology or neuroscience. Others may not want to hear my rants about the job. I purposefully left the book relatively short, as I know how hard it is sometimes to actually get some time to read an entire book. Moreover, I purposefully left references after many of the key points so the reader can refer to the annotated bibliography in the back of the book if they are interested in similar research. In any case, this is a book by a cop, for cops so I talk like a fucking cop. If you are at all sensitive or get offended easily, do yourself a favor and just put the book down now. For the rest of you, please stay open-minded as we take a look at the law enforcement lifestyle like I do...

Chapter 1
FTO OBSERVATIONS

"A pint of sweat will save a gallon of blood."
                                                    -Patton

In 2010, I was involved in an Officer-Involved Shooting (OIS). Even though I have been a hunter all my life and played sports just as long, I did not like how my body felt in that moment. For the first time I felt all the psychological and physiological effects, such as auditory exclusion, tunnel vision, time distortion and memory gaps; which only truly come along with life or death type stress. I still handled business, however it left me asking why my body did what it did, and why it was so surreal. Since then I have educated myself on the topic of neuroscience under stress, and even went back to get a second Master's degree so I could truly delve into the science behind police use of force. As my interest in this topic grew, I also started noticing something about the trainees that were coming through the field training program. Some of the trainees seemed to rely on more of an analytical decision-making process, where others had a more intuitional dominant style.

An example could be seen in how long the decision making process would take on a simple pedestrian stop. Often times the task shifting that takes place on a stop is information overload for the analytical type. From the passenger seat, I could see the wheels turning as they bobbled their way through talking on the radio, figuring out their location, turning on the spot light, driving the car, putting it park, all the while watching the suspect and his hands. Then simply talking to the guy was a hurdle in itself.

After about a night or two of having such a trainee, I would casually ask them if they were good at math. Almost every time the answer would be a "yes", so I knew I was onto something. As for the intuitional types, they would make a pedestrian stop and it was night and day from the analytical trainee. These officers would buzz through the steps, sometimes forgetting such things as the spotlight, just so they could get to talking to the suspect. Sometimes it seemed these types of trainees would make more mistakes but there was more urgency (This age old *speed versus accuracy paradox* will be examined further in later chapters). However I would ask these trainees if they were good at math, and usually it was a resounding, "No."

So I took this information and applied the common cultural belief that the trainees were so-called, "right-brained," and "left-brained." For those of you that are unfamiliar with this terminology, the theory is right brained people are more artistic, creative, kinesthetic and intuitional. Whereas, the left-brainers are more analytical, futuristic and rely less on their intuitions. I ran with this thought process for several trainees, and it seemed to assist in my critique of their actions because I could better explain how their brain processed information. But I have to admit I struggled and still do have a difficult time understanding the analytical types. I have been horrible at math all my life and clearly have an intuitional dominant brain. So when I teach these folks that look at things far different than I do, I have to be careful not to become frustrated in the mental processes they must work through.

I found the left-brainers liked when I provided them with an info diet of sorts and told them to "go by the numbers," so they could look at a traffic stop as a math problem.

I have actually seen trainees that had very analytical jobs like accountant or chemist prior to becoming officers and noted they are as analytical as they come. They were actually found to conduct a mental checklist of sorts while on stops. This is all good until things do not go according to plan. Problems arise when the suspects, as they so often do, throw a monkey wrench into the call and do not go along with the program. The math brainer would then freeze whilst attempting to make logic out of the suspect's often illogical actions. Indeed the analytical dominant brain will always look to put the pieces together so as to come to some sort of conclusion. Moreover, it was almost as if the analytical trainees were always trying to put their decision into words or create some mental model prior to making a decision. This "sense-making," is far too slow for our rapidly evolving world and frankly quite dangerous. After all, police work in general is counter-intuitive. The "normal" person when confronted with fear tries to escape that immediate area quickly and unscathed. But we sheepdog types must confront those fearful situations head on. Some of us do this more than others, but regardless we are expected to grab ahold of that stranger who is not following our commands or run towards the sound of gunfire. Sounds logical, right?

As I explain this concept, I am sure all of us can think of other cops that possess either a math mind or art brain. Where we really see this play out is on the range. As a firearms instructor, I have seen many analytical brains suffer with the shotgun, but excel with the rifle. The reason for this is because the shooting a shotgun is much more an art, and the rifle is more of a surgical science. Even on the handgun courses of fire, I noted the analytical brains would excel on the precision shooting, but were not as quick on the more dynamic courses of fire.

The same analytical type brains I spoke about earlier really proved this theory one day on the range. I set up a course of fire that focused on simple marksmanship. I glued targets that had several rings depicted on them. These rings were the exact size of a .40 bullet hole, so the objective was to try to shoot one round perfectly into the center hole of the ring. Of course the math brains loved this drill because they could take their time and shoot the handgun in an analytical fashion. But when we did another drill later that consisted of shooting two rounds inside a triangle on the chest of a silhouette from the holster in under 2.5 seconds, the results were much different. The same shooters had a terrible time with the *continuity of action* it took to successfully transition through all of those steps and finish it off rapidly point shooting multiple rounds. Which, unfortunately, the latter drill is much more realistic and typical of most police shootings. Below are four killer traits of having the mental rigidity of an analytical brain:

- *Procrastination*: Delaying action due to imperfect information

- *Perfectionism*: Delaying action due to an imperfect plan

- *Analysis Paralysis:* Delaying action by trying to analyze too much information

- *Group Think*: Taking the most tepid action poisoned by the confirmation by the group

(Divine, 2015).

These concepts are a great illustration to one of the main points of this book- Over-analyzation in this business is dangerous. Our minds have to be malleable. If we look at the above descriptions, think about how many calls cops could have handled differently if they did not fall victim to one or all of these. We never have perfect information, a perfect plan, and we freeze if there is there is too much information coming in. With that said, the last concept of Group Think, is more of a leadership concept, but it still shows how we can all get sucked in by that supervisor who is afraid to act, stalls in making decisions, and seeks out the least intrusive course of action. Don't get me wrong, there is a time and place to slow things down, make a plan and execute. But I am speaking more to the quick action needed when the line has already been drawn in the sand and it is time to move. Most decisions in this job are not linear, so why do we train on the range or in the dtac room that way?

I also teach Hunter Safety to young children and they have been great test subjects because they usually have not been taught bad habits before; so everything they do is truly un-bias and pure. While at a Hunter Safety clinic, I took note that some of the young girls were really good at the rifle. Furthermore they were more often than not, left-eye dominant; meaning they closed their right eye to aim the gun. Which is interesting because studies have revealed the dominant eye processes information to the brain fourteen milliseconds faster than the non-dominant eye (Teig, 2015). So in actuality the non-dominant eye is merely playing catch up all the time anyway. When I asked the kids who were good at the rifle if they were good at math, sure enough my theory was confirmed, there was a resounding, "Yes."

And it should be noted, when I ask people if they are good at math, usually people know this answer and have no reason to fudge on it, so they answer honestly. Rarely do I get a half-ass answer, either one is good at math or not. I for one, suck at any sort of math. I suppose this is probably why I understand the so-called right brainers more. As for the little tikes at the shooting clinic, the young boys were more often right eye dominant and enjoyed the shotgun better. The naturals would shoot the flying clay pigeons with little effort. Furthermore, the boys that were left eye dominant did better on the rifle with a scope and, yes, they were better at math. This left me wondering how our minds become more math or art dominant. Is it how we are raised or could it be genetics? Or perhaps a little of both?

As I read more and more about the left brain hemispheres and right brain hemispheres, I started to discover that my theory was not so simple. Many of the studies that have been done on the hemispheres were done on patients with some sort of medical problem such as epilepsy. Also the experiments were conducted in controlled laboratory environments; not at all like the streets that cops are making decisions on all day and night. Moreover, there are a great majority of scientists out there that dismiss the whole right brain/left brain theory all together, stating that the human brain works together to make decisions and there is no one particular area involved. I can agree somewhat to this, but based on my research, I would argue that for the purposes of rapid decision making like cops use, the brain uses more of the front and middle of their brains so as to make decisions. Now I realize this may spark a debate in the psychology and neuroscience world, but that is my intent. If we can better understand the human brain and science behind why cops do certain things, we can better educate our officers as well as the public.

After I drop a theory bomb like that, I suppose I better explain myself further. First off, it is well known that cops must make rapid decisions under the great stress of life or death. I am not limiting my scope of decision making strictly to officer-involved shootings however. When thinking about these topics, please ponder the simple act of going hands on to effect an arrest as well. Because no matter the call for service, there is always at least one gun involved (ours) and there is always an inherent need to take control of the unknowns quickly. With that said, what many people do not realize is most cops are making decisions every day with their mid-brain, or what I like to call their caveman brain. In a rapid stressful environment, cops do not always have time to cognitively explore all their options to make decisions. In fact, often times the word decision cannot accurately be used to explain what has occurred because that implies they thought about what they were doing at the time prior to acting. Rather, they acted and may have only had time for a flash option to pop into their heads before taking action. Action beats reaction every time. This is why Officers cannot always wait for a crook to point the gun at them, because by then it is too late. At that point, the mid-brain is acting based on the age-old "fight, flight or freeze," response. There is no cognitive thought, which is what admin and the media want. The caveman brain is what we have used for thousands of years and it is better known as our "gut instinct," our natural reaction to someone trying to hurt us. The front of our minds have developed greatly over time, however the sad truth is the fight or flight portion of our brains that has sustained us for thousands of years has changed very little as we have evolved.

So when I observe a rookie Officer in a new environment such as the concrete jungle, it is very easy to see their behavior revert very quickly to the cave man times.

Thus, as trainers we must examine what we can do to fast-forward their learning curve so as to reach the cognitive, rapid thinking of a more senior officer. But first we must start with why.

This job is all about experience. There is a reason when cops talk about a senior salt, we mention how long he's been a cop or the amount of years he spent in a particular unit. We all realize that exposure is the name of the game, but why? I can sum it up in one word: *intuition.* Cops that have seen more shit are able to see several steps ahead, so in-turn they are less stressed. Moreover, because they are able to see the bigger picture, they are able to suck up more stimulus (information) from their environment. Or perhaps filter through the less important stuff and hyper-focus on what needs to be addressed. We have all seen how that senior salt show up on a call and almost magically figure out what is going on and defuse it quickly and calmly; meanwhile the rook is still trying to figure out how to pull up to the scene properly. The senior guy is acting on his gut feelings that he has drawn from experience- intuition. But these new hires are lacking this big time. So we must expose these rookies to as much as we can so as to build up their experience and intuition. But there is one more observation that I have made that may muddy the waters further.

As stated before, most people have a more dominant style of decision making, whether it be analytical or intuitional. To parallel with that, the analytical types are inherently better at mathematics. As a result, they are usually better at such tasks as booking evidence properly and reconstructing traffic collisions. Meanwhile, The intuitional types are usually better at talking to people and report writing.

My guess for this is the analytical type person likes things to be logical, linear and in-order, whereas the intuitional person relies more on their imagination and gut-feeling. Now, I am not trying to get all warm and fuzzy, but imagination is vital to our success as cops.

First, part of the reason why the aforementioned salty cop can see into the future with great precision is because he can imagine what is going to occur. Imagination allows us to begin with the end in mind. And in the world of use of force, the end truly does justify the means. For example, if I am talking to suspect on a ped-stop and dispatch advises he has a warrant. At this point, I know he is going to jail so that decision has been made for me. But he decides to not go along with the program and starts to walk away. As I grab his arm, he tenses up and pulls towards the center of his body. I feel this *proprioception*, and react. Notice I say react and not make the decision to act. Now this is the very small point of time in my mind that I want to explore deeper. Most cops that I have spoken to do not realize how they get to the next step, i.e., leg sweep, elbow, arm-bar take down. However, based on my own experience, our "decision-making process" is much more fast and dirty than we realize. What happens is we actually have a "flash decision" or "snap decision." For me, the toolbox in my brain will quickly toss up my next move (based on past experience) and I will either engage using a technique that popped into my head or shake it off much like a pitcher telling a catcher no to the fastball. If I mentally shake the technique off, then I must reach into my other limited amount of bag of tricks for that particular event in a limited amount of time- less than 300 milliseconds to be exact. Appraisal of the situation requires mental activity involving judgement, discrimination and choice of activity based on past experience (Hammond, 2000).

But what if we do not have prior experience to be drawn from? Fact is in a novel experience, we draw from our human gut that has allowed us to survive for thousands of years. And this is the process that no one outside of the business will ever fucking understand. But getting back to the guy with the warrant. Say my flash decision is to hit him in the back of the head with my baton. Obviously I would have to shake that off, and have another flash decision that better suits that particular situation. It may seem extreme, but this is exactly how cops end up on the news. Their flash decision to act does not exactly fit the call or does not look pretty. But that move or technique was what popped into their head at that time, under stress. The fact is, we humans are inherently lazy, including our minds. Individuals do not search for the most optimal choices but instead, due to time constraints and limited computational capacity, we seek solutions which satisfies our level of aspiration and then our mind terminates any further search. That said, the aspiration to survive can have a lot of emotion attached to it, in-turn making snap judgements that much more extreme. This "weighing," of contingencies can be exacerbated because cops have to always think the worst, which is inherently bias. A decision maker attends to both the expected costs (primarily the mental energy required to implement the strategy) and expected benefits (the ability of the strategy to make the best choice). Within this decision making process it is proposed that people will choose the strategy that maximizes coherence while minimizing effort. In sticking with our brains being lazy, if we have multiple available strategies which are more or less accurate, we will adopt the one that requires the least effort, but is in-turn the most efficient (Hammond, 2000). This is why after the fact, some people may look at a decision and think 2+2=4, however in actuality the decision-maker's process was more like 1+1+1+1=4. This is called the "principle of invariance," Essentially, much like administrators, this principle demands that judgements should remain the same regardless of the presentation of the problem (2000). Thus further illustrating my point that administrators and society simply do not realize that more often than not, cops are making decisions, strike that, reacting with the first judgement that occurs in their caveman brain. This portion of our brains that has been around the longest and has served us quite well. In my opinion, however the problem with modern society is that we have gotten far away from the need for this portion of the brain, also known as the limbic system. Rather, most people in today's society have time to analyze and interpret nearly every decision they make. In fact, in the business world it is damn near expected. We as a people have evolved so much that we are getting away from our innate survival instincts and are strictly relying on the frontal part of our brain to get us through life.

I would rather have a flash decision than an analytical one and I will explain why. It all goes back to that balance between speed and accuracy. We do not have time to waste and seconds truly do matter. Trust me, there is time to analyze a situation, but in terms of most use of force incidents, the faster stimulus is processed and countered, the faster resolve to the situation there is. The longer we are in conflict, the more likely both sides are going to get hurt. I have watched some of my analytical dominant officers allow a suspect to move around, put their hands in their pockets or outright go for a weapon, and, because of the lull in their decision making process, the situation was able to evolve into something larger than it needed be. Even after being on the street for some time, I do not believe one cannot rid themselves of their inherent decision-making style. I have seen the analytical dominant officers develop their skills in talking to people and report writing, but it is very difficult for them to overcome the habit of exploring all of their options prior to acting.

Because that is what analyzing is, examining all options, picking out the best one, and coming to a decision. However, one can clearly see the accuracy of the decision may be better, but the suspect might have moved on to a whole new problem before that one is solved. Time is of the essence, and cops must rely on their rapid flash decisions so as to overcome resistance prior to becoming another statistic.

I have noticed that most of the new hires have never played sports or have very limited experience in the rapid decision making needed in sports. After all, we are all police athletes. We drive fast, shoot, run (maybe), jump and practice martial arts. But these are relatively foreign concepts to the new hires, who often times haven't played too many sports. So we trainers are truly starting from scratch in terms of athletic decision making and motor programming. Furthermore, because they have grown up in a world that is ever-germ conscious, there is clear personal bubble that must not be violated. It is a hurdle for us to overcome when trainees are not used to touching another person. After all, they would be expelled from school for a shoving match in school, so heaven forbid they even want to get close to a smelly transient, let alone grapple on the ground with him. I have noticed this even in Field Training orientation, where I teach Defensive Tactics. These trainees are hesitant to touch me or another cop, so there is obviously an even larger hesitation to go hands with crooks. Also along those same lines, there is a lack of new hires that never hunted or spent much time outdoors. In my opinion, hunting game is the best practice we can get for quickly assessing our environment and scanning for potential threats. Also, anyone who has suffered from "buck fever," realizes the great importance of controlling breathing. We learn the fundamentals of marksmanship under stress and tactical breathing.

Moreover, the exposure to weapons manipulations makes us that much more proficient with the tools of our trade. So I understand if someone did not grow up in a hunting family, I get it. But any type of sport would benefit someone who wants to be a professional observer for a living. With that said, one attribute that in a way ties this chapter together is vision.

I do not know what is in the water nowadays, but it seems there is great abundance of new hires that have horrible vision. Granted they all wear contacts or glasses, but I never realized how much my eyesight has helped me in sports, hunting and in the job until I had some of these trainees in my car. So it is a potentially deadly combination of having terrible vision coupled with the slow stimulus processing that so many of our new cops suffer from. It should be noted, my observations and research on vision was another reason behind the name of this book. In fact, sometimes I feel like Paul Newman said in the classic movie, Butch Cassidy and the Sundance Kid, "I got vision, and the rest of the world wears bifocals" (1969).

The best partner I'll ever have.

Chapter 2
Behind Blue Eyes

"A good plan violently executed now is better than a perfect plan executed next week."

-Patton

According to the National Law Enforcement Officers Memorial Fund (NLEOMF) web page, (2017, April, http://nleomf.com/), from 2006-2015, 545 American Police Officers were shot, stabbed, beaten or strangled. Another 478 died in vehicle collisions, and 128 were struck by a vehicle (2017).

Some would argue the violence towards law enforcement is part of the "Ferguson Effect," which is a largely debatable term that has not yet been clearly defined or confirmed. In essence, it can be either viewed as the increased scrutiny of police actions and use of force, or the increase in crime because law enforcement has become less proactive in the wake of highly criticized political events (Beckett, 2016). Much like anything else, the Ferguson Effect can be viewed differently depending on what side of the political fence one stands. However, one thing is for certain, the Ferguson Effect has claimed many lives and destroyed property, thus there is clearly a need for Officers to be peak performers so as to safely protect themselves and the community to which they serve (MacDonald, 2016).

Coincidently, as the criminals in society are becoming more aggressive, the new generation of cops are getting softer. "Millennials," born between 1980 and 2000 (Corgnet & Espin, 2016), grew up in a generation of active parents with a great emphasis placed on safety, nurturing and technology.

In-turn, because of the dependence upon their parents, the millennials have never truly developed their decision-making skills (Bland, Melton, Welle & Bigham, 2008). Moreover, a lack of sports coupled with the technological upbringing, the Millennial brain has evolved to be far more analytical versus intuitional in its decision-making. (Okoli, Weller & Watt, 2015). Thus, the contemporary workforce lacks the rapid split-second decision-making needed in law enforcement and there is more of a need for psychoeducation and mental skills training than ever before.

Because police athletes make life or death decisions within milliseconds of time in violent, rapidly evolving, dynamic situations, it is vital that they receive better psychoeducational training. Mental skills techniques such as visualization are more than helpful in developing their instinctual decision-making process so as to make quick decisions more safely. To that end, law enforcement trainers must focus on teaching new hires the neuroscience behind rapid decision-making, as well as developing the intuition of the millennial generation of Police Officers.

My empirical research spans across several disciplines, ranging from the evolution of the relatively new field of neuroscience, to include right and left brain hemispheric processing, ventral and dorsal processing, bottom-up and top-down processing, and lastly mid-brain and frontal lobe processing (Dew, 1996, Orr, 2011, Vickers, 2011, Gilbert, 2013, Sukel, 2016). The research then takes the information gained from those domains and applies it to the rapid decision-making needed in high risk professions like law enforcement.

It is my intent to simplify the many idiosyncrasies of neuroscience and examine the research that has already been conducted within other domains such as sport. Concurrently, the need for performance psychoeducation and mental skills techniques are also illustrated, along with the exploration of the benefits for "Millennial," officers to learn to be more intuitional versus analytical in their decision making.

I am going to preface the rest of this chapter by warning the reader; this subject matter may seem all too scientific, but I believe it is important to know as professionals. In the end, this job is all about experience, so knowing the psychology behind what we do makes us better witnesses, which means we write better reports, and in-turn we are better clients in the courtroom. Also, we will be able to better identify the many natural effects of use of force during an actual incident.

John Dew wrote an article simply titled, "Are you a right brain or a left brain thinker?" (1996). This article can be viewed as somewhat outdated, however it still provides the reader with the fundamental base behind the right and left brain theory. It should be also noted, the initial intent of this research was to determine if there was any validity to the exact same question Dew proposed in the article. Dew wrote about initial brain hemispheric research done by Nobel Prize winner, Roger Sperry, who established that, "The left side of the brain deals with a problem or situation by collecting data, making analyses, and using a rational thinking process to reach a logical conclusion. The right side of the brain approaches the same problem or situation by making intuitive leaps to answers based on insight and perceptions (Dew, 1996)."

Sperry's research clearly illustrated the differences and provided historical research to show validity. However, Terence Hines wrote an article in 2003 titled, "Left Brain, Right Brain: Who's on First?" This article completely attempted to destroy the idea behind the left and right brain concept and called it a "myth" (Hines, 2003). Yet another more recent article titled, "Left and right brain-oriented hemisity subjects show opposite behavioral preferences," (2012), went away from the traditional binary "Hemisphericity," concept and now states that "Hemisity," is where each individual is either left or right brain-oriented with no intermediates possible (2012). Such articles provide the researcher with information on both theories and are based on mostly research data and expert opinion. However it should be noted, according to author and researcher, Michael Gazzaniga, who wrote "Tales From Both Sides of the Brain, A Life in Neuroscience, (2015); many of the split-brain experiments Sperry and other neuroscience researchers, including Gazzaniga himself, conducted were on animals such as rats, as well as humans with epilepsy. These landmark studies become important in illustrating the arguments against a clearly defined split brained human decision making process. "Split-brain patients," are people who have had surgery or trauma to certain portions of the brain, and have been the source of an abundance of research hemispheric tendencies (Marinsek, Turner, Gazzaniga, & Miller, 2014). Through this research the authors have concluded the left hemisphere tends to create explanations, make inferences, and attempt to bridge gaps of information; while the right hemisphere tends to detect conflict, update beliefs, support mental set-shifts, and monitor and inhibit behavior (2014).

This information provided the research with clear and updated information of the obvious differences of the hemispheres. The authors went on to illustrate that even though the left hemisphere has the ability to explain, it is only as good as the information it receives. As in police use of force, a rapidly evolving situation, most often the information is short and lacks abundance; thus the left brain may create explanations that are incorrect, inappropriate or even bizarre. In conclusion, with healthy patients, it was shown that lateralized processing in the brain maximizes brain efficiency and increases processing speed. The authors state, "In sum, we suggest that, in the domain of inferential reasoning, the left hemisphere strives to reduce uncertainty while the right hemisphere strives to resolve inconsistency. The hemispheres' divergent inferential reasoning strategies may contribute to flexible, complex reasoning in the healthy brain, and disruption in these systems may explain reasoning deficits in the unhealthy brain, (2014)." In other words, if a decision maker can learn to use both hemispheres by "dual-processing," it will reduce redundancy in the overall decision making process. This is an important concept to note, because in law enforcement our minds must be able to change with the incoming stimulus, as well as process it, all in the interest of time.

Decision-making models

In the article, "Information processing and intuitive decision-making on the fire ground: towards a model of expert intuition, (Okoli, Weller & Watt, 2015), the authors illustrated a qualitative study carried out with sixteen experienced fire commanders. The objectives of this paper were (1) to present and discuss a decision-making model, the information filtering and intuitive decision-making model, which describes how experts actually make decisions in a volatile, uncertain, complex and ambiguous (VUCA) environment and (2) to compare and contrast the information filtering and intuitive decision model (IFID) with other decision-making models, and to discuss the implications of the model for research and practice. In the research, the authors were able to measure reaction times via interviews with the fire commanders following a high stress incident. The majority of decisions during the fire were "intuitive," and made in less than a minute. Some decisions combined both intuition and analytical thinking but those decisions were made over some length of time and from prior experience (2015). In reading this, one can see some of the similarities and differences between the decisions made by police officers and firefighters. However, it should be noted a police officer does not always have the luxury of time during a primal decision to act, such as during the "fight flight or freeze," mode that often is involved with police encounters during an altercation or threatening incident, (Gluck, 2007).

Authors Raab and Laborde wrote, "When to Blink and When to Think: Preference for Intuitive Decisions Results in Faster and Better Tactical Choices (2011)." Even though the word "tactical," was chosen for this title, it was meant for a sport setting, but can still apply to tactical decisions made by law enforcement. This peer-reviewed article takes the theory of people having deliberate and intuitional decision-making preferences and actually provides a few different definitions from a management, psychology and sport lens. The article explores why it is hypothesized, those who are more intuitional make faster decisions under time constraints. Moreover the authors supply the researcher with a need for mental imagery so as to create maximum exposure to information processing, which is what separates the expert from the novice (2011). All in all, this study proved "less is more," when it comes to making a decision in a high risk event. Moreover, the fire commander observations illustrated the importance of training and experience so as to make a more intuitive decision, which limits the valuable time it takes to make a more analytical decision. The authors stated, "In complex environments where complex tasks are required to be performed amidst incomplete information and time pressure, intuition is most likely to be more effective than analytical/deliberative strategies. The intuitive mode, designed to process information quicker and therefore possessing a higher capacity, is more appropriate in time-pressured environments, (Okoli, Weller & Watt, 2015)."

However as stated in the article, "Cortico-striatal connections predict control over speed and accuracy in perceptual decision making," the authors stated, "For many everyday life decisions, people and animals face the dilemma that fast decisions tend to be error-prone, whereas accurate decisions tend to be relatively slow. In other words, the temporal benefits of responding quickly come at a cost of increased error rates, a phenomenon known as the speed–accuracy tradeoff (Forstmann, 2010)"

This speed-accuracy trade-off can be the source of many second guessed decisions, a trade-off that can be the difference between life and death.

Speed/ Accuracy Trade Off

Researchers have found there is a classic tradeoff between speed and accuracy and this is the fundamental difference between left brain and right brain thinking or analytical and intuitional decision-making. On one hand, pre-cognitive reactions are faster, but not always the "best," option; whereas cognitive decisions are slower, but most obvious options are analyzed and concluded. The larger question we are left with is which is "better," for law enforcement? Speed or Accuracy? Or do police athletes need both; and must learn when to utilize one or the other, when to react and when to respond?

This concept is huge but rarely touched on in law enforcement circles. Just like in sports, the better play may be for the short stop to throw home instead of going for the easy out at first. However, the emotions involved over losing the World Series versus someone dying in a police action, or lack thereof, clearly has much greater consequences. Subsequently, officers must find balance between a quick decision and the best decision for those circumstances. I recall one morning after working all night, I was asked to assist with a search warrant in a neighboring agency for the nearby drug task force. After searching two homes for dope with my dog, my agency asked for a K-9 to assist with a residential burglary in progress. I hauled ass over there and contacted the primary officer. He told me a male was seen going through a back window of an apartment complex and he had not come out.

The neighbors were sure they did not know him and believed the home owners were gone. Based on this, I gave a loud K-9 announcement near an open window at the front of the residence. There was no answer, so my search team made entry. Soon thereafter, I heard another officer yelling in the back at someone to show his hands. Thinking the suspect was now trying to escape, I exited the apartment with my dog and started to run outside. But then that other officer yelled that he went back into the same window. I gave another announcement at the narrow hallway that led to three closed doors. I confirmed which room he was in and tried the door but it was locked. I then began trying to kick the door down. Because of the small hallway, I was unable to get a good kick and my attempts were unsuccessful. I then backed away and gave yet another announcement for him to come out. I saw the door crack open and saw the dude look right at me, but then he quickly shut the door. Given the suspect's behavior, I then kicked the door in and sent my dog in the room to safely apprehend the suspect. However, once I got in there I noticed he was bare footed and had pajama pants on. Long story short, dude came home late and apparently forgot his keys so he broke in to the room he was renting. I ended up getting sued, but this case supplies us with a prime example of speed versus accuracy.

Unfortunately, cops do not always have all the information, or even the correct information at the time of a call. And because calls happen so quickly and generally sporadic, we do not always have the time to downshift. In my case, we could not afford the time for a burglary suspect to barricade himself and potentially arm himself. Thus, with limited knowledge we had at the time, we made the more rapid, but some would argue the less accurate decision to make entry. Hindsight is always 20/20 and it is for this reason Graham v. Connor exists.

Like stated previously, usually our guts are right because our intuition has been developed over thousands of years. All too often, we must get out of our own way to draw on this experience because our frontal brain wants to make linear decisions according to the logical script. With that said, with not all officers reacting the same way nowadays in certain situations, it has become more difficult to definitively prove that a "like" officer would make the same decision, given the same set of facts and circumstances.

If we have to judge the distance of an object, we simply do it. Think about picking a coffee cup up off the kitchen table. We do not have to think about it or how to do it. Such a task does not require intelligence, thought, memory, training, awareness of the process or ability other than that was given to us biologically. In order to achieve empirical accuracy, the task requires that we possess some sort of knowledge (cues are important), experience (accuracy in reading cues), and perhaps thought, depending on whether the task is intuitional or analytical. And lastly, the task may force us to employ a specific organizational method such as pattern recognition (Hammonds, 2000). These points further illustrate the complexity of finding a balance between speed and accuracy. Paradoxically, we can very well be accurate but too slow to be effective. Or we can be too fast, and suffer the aftermath of being less accurate.

"System 1" and "System 2" Cognition

"The subcortical brain responds to simply, to simple stimuli, without much in the way of conscious, cognitive activity. The cortex responds in a more complex, mediated, cognitive way ("Processing Under Pressure, Stress, Memory and Decision-Making in Law Enforcement," Matthew Sharps, 2010)." Thus illustrating the point that instead of the so-called "right or left brain thinking," neurologists have now proven that under stress the brain actually has a division of labor, both in an analytical and intuitional fashion, or as author Daniel Kahneman who wrote, "Thinking Fast and Slow, (2011) referred to as 'system 1' and 'system 2' thinking." He describes 'system 1,' as "fast; it's intuitive, associative, metaphorical, automatic, impressionistic, and it can't be switched off." System 1 sounds a lot like the intuitional "right," brain. Whereas, the 'system 2,' is described as, "System 2 is slow, deliberate, and effortful. Its operations require attention." Thus, one can see System 1 is more autonomic, whereas System 2 is more cognitive; echoing the previous theory of left brain and right brain thinkers.

Hogarth, the author of, "Intuition: A Challenge for Psychological Research on Decision Making, (2010)," describes the systems as "experiential," and "rational," or "tacit," and "deliberate." She conducted a qualitative study that illustrated the subjective phenomenon of intuition and how difficult it is to gauge by researchers. She defines intuition as, "the use of knowledge that cannot be made explicit but is surprising-if not a little magical- in its accuracy Moreover, she believes most human decisions are comprised of more of a "dual process thinking," but admits it is all a matter of degree (2010).

Now imagine the reluctance to this concept by administrators who want everything black and white. I suppose this paradox is the root cause of the mysterious world of law enforcement use of force. On one hand, rapid intuitional decision making is desired and needed. However, on the other hand it is far too complex and unpredictable to be relied upon. In other words, when officers are making a decision, the degree to which intuition plays a role is much more than when making a basic decision to eat when hungry. Moreover, in many natural settings there is no obvious analytical model to which decisions can be made, but rather intuition is the only recourse for reaction (2010). In-turn, "Training programs should help novices in building mental models and make results of recognition based decision-making routines explicit so that they can be refined (Chauvin, 2009)."

"Reflection in Action"

"Reflection-in-action," (Heuvel, Alison & Power, 2014) refers to the self-monitoring or intuitive reflection that allows for uncertainty to become more manageable by framing the problem. By eliminating the psychological noise within one's thoughts, the decision maker can focus on what is most important at that given time. This *"mental noise,"* is an important topic to delve deeper into. We have all fell victim to it one way or the other. If you have ever turned down the music in the car because you were lost, then you were subconsciously attempting to limit the noise going on inside your brain. But what administrators and the media do not understand is just how often this chatter happens during a high stress incident.

Often times when officers are interviewed after their officer involved shootings, more often than not they will comment on a thought that traveled through their minds that did not exactly fit into the incident. One officer I spoke to stated he had the odd thought that a subject was pointing a toy gun at him, and the officer even asked himself, "Why is this guy messin with me?" This thought was quickly dismissed and he went on to shoot the culprit who was in actuality attempting to ambush him with an assault rifle while he was trying to enjoy a warm cup in a coffee shop. The scary part of these random thoughts is that they take time, sometimes precious time, that could be vital. This is a great time to also address another all too common phenomenon that occurs under great stress, which is priming. This is somewhat of a psychological term, but it really does apply to police work.

When Officers get into shootings, one of the questions the investigators will ask is if that Officer responded to any violent calls recently or if anything bothered him emotionally. An example would maybe be a call where an infant died or there was a close call with a man with a gun. Subconsciously, we humans store this in our memory bank. And although cops are usually really good at compartmentalizing, these experiences still seep into our thought processes. I remember after my shooting, I went to the grocery store a few days later. While I was walking out of the store into the crowded parking lot, a soccer mom was not paying attention and failed to yield for me right away. I wouldn't say she almost hit me, but she was heading that way is all. This is a pretty common occurrence for anyone, but it was like I was threatened with deadly force all over again. Time stopped, my body tensed up, palms got sweaty, and my head felt like it shrunk in. Oh, and I reached for my right hip. These reactions were all before I had time to even process what was occurring. Once I did make eye contact with the driver and realized this very brief moment was just my subconscious mind reacting to a primed stimulus, I shook it off and was able to keep walking to my car. With this story in mind, we can see that often times we can head into calls without even realizing we are already primed to react a certain way. And if those memories make their way into our cognitive recall, then the reaction will be that much stronger because that mental chatter made us aware of it both intuitionally and analytically.

Another example of mental noise I have heard was when an officer was involved in a shootout and actually took the time to think the suspect was throwing beer cans at him, however it was later determined they were actually his .45 casings going by him in ultra-slow speed. I too fell victim of useless mental chatter during an off-duty incident.

I was heading pig hunting with my father one early morning and stopped off for a cup of joe at the local 7-11. As we pulled up, I noticed a dude with his right hand in his hoodie pocket and seemed to be having an argument with the clerk. I was armed with my .45 on my hip and decked out in full camo, so I walked in to get my coffee and to investigate further. At one point, I heard the crook asking the clerk, "Oh you're gonna GIVE that to me, huh?" Soon I stepped up to the counter with my items and the suspect let me go in front of him. Again, another red flag that something was amiss. I looked out of the corner of my eye and saw a silver object in his right hand that was in the hoodie, so then I knew a robbery was going down. I thought about launching my attack right then and there, but decided against it. Instead, I walked out to our vehicle and told my dad to call 9-11.

I said, tell the dispatcher the 7-11 is getting robbed and the dude in all camo armed with an AR is an off-duty cop. That's right, remember I was going pig hunting, so I retrieved my AR10 and waited until dude came out of the store. When he did, I yelled at him to show me his hands and ordered him to the ground. As he somewhat complied, I remembered worrying that I did not have all of this on recording. Yea, even though I was off-duty, the write ups I had received from my department for not turning on my recorder scarred me so much that it surfaced at that intense moment.

Luckily, such irrelevant self-talk did not hinder my capability to handle business, but I believe this is the type of second-guessing supervisors and the media are causing in our cops. In-turn, cops are becoming more and more analytical in their decision-making, not realizing they are gambling with vital time. In analytical thought, there is a tendency to 'widen' available information which may in-turn cause "seizing and freezing" (2014).

Thus, it can be concluded rather than pointlessly deliberating between options (analyzing) without actively reducing uncertainty not only uses valuable time, but also can be considered a maladaptive coping strategy.

Ventral and Dorsal Systems

According to one of the leading researchers of Police Force Science, William Lewinski, in an article titled, "Performing Under Pressure: Gaze control, decision making and shooting performance of elite and rookie police officers, (Vickers & Lewinski, 2011)," he states, "The ventral system (left hemisphere) is the slower of the two systems and facilitates the reorienting of attention and cognitive processing. The dorsal system (right hemisphere) is designed to control fast actions that are controlled automatically. Vickers and Lewinski point out that performers can utilize both systems throughout an event, but novice's heavy reliance on either can inevitably affect their performance (2011). Now if we think about that for a moment from a vision standpoint, the novice is using up a lot more time and energy just to process the incoming information that they are seeing with their eyes. Whereas, the expert is using up less time and energy to filter through what is unimportant visually, and in-turn is provided with more focus on what is important at that particular moment in time.

In the article, "Top-Down influences on visual processing," the author defines "top-down," as the cognitive influences and higher order representations that impinge upon earlier steps in information processing. Thus, the opposite of such processing would naturally be "bottom-up processing."

Such literature refers to the cortical areas used when visually processing stimulus. If one can picture an image of a human brain from the side of the head, this concept makes more sense. It should be noted, such is similar to the concepts behind right-brain and left-brain processing where essentially top-down processing is more analytical whereas bottom-up is more instinctual.

However instead of viewing the brain from the top of the head, from a side view, this concept suggests the brain processes information quickly from the bottom up, however as time goes on, the brain can cognitively process information slower with the top of the brain. Then the information travels back down through the brain, into the spinal cord and to the rest of the body where we can react physically to the incoming information. It truly is amazing to think all of this happens in just milliseconds without us truly having to think about most actions. Thus, visual processing, reaction time and movement time make up the often overlooked, but vitally important part of use of force. We will explore visual processing in greater detail in the following chapter.

Conscious and Sub-Conscious

Naturalistic Decision Making (NDM) is another framework of intuitional processing the fight or flight dynamic that law enforcement, firefighters and military personnel face during a deadly threat. Otherwise known as the sub-conscious and conscious reactions to a threat, including the emotional aspects such as fear, and the theory of 'bottom up cognition' (Rahamm, 2009). Author Rahamm explores the evolution of the human mind and how we still have the same innate bias towards survival. The question is if the body reacts to the felt emotions or the scary stimulus first? The NDM serves as a nexus between natural, emotional and cognitive decision making as it pertains to tactical decision making.

To put this into context, nearly everyone has had a close call while traveling in a car. Maybe a kid chases a ball into the street and the driver has to slam on the brakes to avoid hitting the unsuspecting child. At this split-second, we experience the tunnel vision- but the accelerated heart rate, clammy hands and shortness of breath only come after the car stops and the kid goes running off unscathed. This is because our body does not have time to react to the emotion, rather only just the stimulus. It is only once things slow down that we react to our emotions and the cognitive thought of the disaster that was just avoided. Our conscious is what provides us with the "if-then" equation and the many emotions associated with what "could" have been. This level of cognitive thought is what makes us uniquely human. My K9 partner functions with his subconscious mind and he would never go to bite my Sergeant and think, "If I bite the wrong person, then I will be in trouble." He is not capable of such reasoning.

Now granted, my dog is smarter than many of the cops I know, but I am sure we all have done stuff on-duty when we did not think of the consequences of our actions in an "if-then," fashion. We usually come out okay on the other end, but I am sure after reading this book, the reader will better recognize just how often we are acting subconsciously (especially administrators).

In a book review of "Blink: The Power of Thinking without Thinking, (Gladwell, 2005)," and "Strangers to Ourselves: Discovering the Adaptive Unconscious (Wilson, 2002)," author Spike Cramphorn, explores the unconscious and conscious in a response to both books; namely how most of our reactions (decisions) are initiated by unconscious, feelings-based interpretations. Moreover, Wilson is quoted in saying, "The term "adaptive unconscious," recognizes that nonconscious thinking was an evolutionary adaptation that gave a quick response survival advantage. However, the consciousness, and the ability to rationalize evolved much later (Wilson, 2002). In other words, our 'primitive' brain that is considered inferior to the conscious brain, is actually paramount to our survival. Cramphorn elaborates and states, "Our 'gut-feelings,' are a conscious physiological discernment of an unconscious mental reaction (2006)." Such outside awareness thinking illustrates how often we rely on our initial instincts to an uneasy situation, much like our ancestors did years before. However, the question must be asked if the millennial generation has evolved so much, have they lost these primal instincts necessary to survival?

Relying on gut feelings can be a scary proposition for those stakeholders within the criminal justice field that have a desire to make policy as non-subjective as possible.

But there has been research conducted that may shed some light on the accuracy of intuition. Dr. Landers, from Arizona State University, recorded the brain waves of Olympic shooters and the accuracy of their shots (Lewinski, 2002). By examining the brain waves, Landers was able to determine the more the shooter was dissociated, focused and relaxed, the more accurate the shot was. Whereas, the shooter who was distracted by thoughts or feelings, shot more poorly (2002). The message from this research is if an officer cannot dissociate or remove his conscious mind from the presence of a lethal threat- his trained, tactical skills can suffer drastically (2002). To this end, in later chapters we will discuss performance psychology skills to overcome such mental chatter and explain how to quiet the mind for better performance.

In the book, "The Art of Risk, The New Science of Courage, Caution, and Chance, (2016)" Sukel provides the reader with updated and contemporary views in neuroscience and psychology. The topic of the flight or fight center in the brain (amygdala), and the frontal lobe are portions of the brain that are pinnacle to my research. Moreover, those two portions suggest that within the 300 milliseconds it takes to react to a threat, we are not thinking with either our right or left hemispheres, rather our mid-brain is reacting and the fore-brain does the thinking. For the purpose of the research, this 300 milliseconds is the portion of time most in question. It should be noted, rather than the aforementioned theory of hemispheric decision making, this updated research now suggests humans react and make decisions in more of a mid-brain and frontal fashion (Sukel, 2016). This is huge. Essentially our mid-brain is the ancient intuitional brain, whereas the frontal lobe is our human analytical brain.

Millennial Decision-Making

It is believed the Millennial generation's higher level of parent involvement may inhibit their epistemological development (Pizzolato & Hicklen, 2011). Epistemological is basically a fancy word for the theory of knowledge. Increased dependence is linked to a lack of critical thinking skills and identity development. Such major developmental hurdles result in a lack of life experience, a lack of the ability to solve problems, make decisions and make sense of a novel situation (2011). Also communication through technology such as cell phones, text messages, and email have created a "conned," environment (Bland et. al, 2009). What this means is not only has our world become smaller, but technology has become not only the norm, but expected by young people. Thus, researchers have attempted to determine ways to develop better coping mechanisms for the millennial college population (2009). For the purpose of this book, the nexus will be made between such Millennials and the incoming generation to police work.

Based on empirical research and literature review, it is important to note there has been little research on how the theories of analytical and intuitional decision making affect the police athlete's decision making under threat. Moreover, with the highly technological millennial generation coming into the workforce, the need for performance psychology techniques and the development of intuition must take place early on in police training, such as in the academy and in the field training program.

The contemporary consensus is that there is no one side of the brain or the other that solely makes decisions (Bien & Sack, 2014). Rather, the brain has many working parts and depending upon the stimulus, some parts can be more dominant. To that end, it is unknown if someone is born a "right brain thinker," or "left brain thinker," or if they develop such cognitive style over time and through experience. But through research, it has been found that there is still some validity that some people are more primed to rely on more of an analytical or intuitive style of decision-making; and utilize more dominant neurobiological hemispheres in certain situations. More rigorous, scientific research would further show the advantages of either, and allow educators, trainers and supervisors to create better curriculum. Also they could design better training programs because they will better understand how the mind learns and processes information under stress. Through exploratory qualitative research it is recognized there are limitations to the current research on this important area of hemispheric analytical and intuitional decision-making in a high risk environment. While it is true there has been much analysis and literature about the topic, some of the research is speculative; thus causing some question in the research's internal and external validity. This is mainly due to the lack of data that can be collected in an actual high risk situation versus a laboratory setting. Participants in future studies will have to wear a portable 'fMRI' machine so as to illustrate where their brain neurons are activated during a high stress police incident, as well other technology such as a heart rate monitor (Marinsek, Turner, Gazzaniga, & Miller, 2014). Furthermore, there can be inherent "memory gaps," during a high stress event so many of the decisions that are made pre-cognitively cannot be recalled in post-incident interviews (Schwabe, 2013).

Through content analysis, this research was able to ask some much needed questions about hemispheric processing and the pros and cons of analytical/intuitional decision-making in regard to how each function in a dynamic law enforcement use of force; as well as establish strong phenomenon patterns.

Countless documents and experiments have illustrated the various decision-making styles and what parts of the brain are stimulated during each. And although more scientific research is yet to be done to further confirm the many theories of neuroscience, it is evident that two decision-making styles are most common; analytical and intuitional or slow and fast. (Okoli, Weller & Watt, 2015). Moreover, it has been clearly shown that the element of speed versus accuracy is all subjective based on the context. As for a law enforcement use of force, few if any, natural-setting experiments have been conducted so as to truly and scientifically confirm any real life speeds and variables (Raab & Laborde, 2011). The two main findings are that every human, not just police officers, make decisions based on the stimulus presented to them physiologically. However, as noted previously, many of our reactions are done so unconsciously or pre-cognitively. This 'thin-slicing (Gladwell, 2005),' enables humans to not have to ponder every decision throughout the day and allows us to make decisions without taking the time to really think about them. It is unknown at this point if a perfectly healthy brain is completely dominated by one style or the other, left or right, analytical or intuitional. But the findings in the literature show that as it pertains to police use of force, sports or any other fear based response, the mid-brain or limbic system dominates rapid/dynamic decision making.

The brain's autonomic responses in a rapidly evolving-time crunched event allow for that decision maker to quickly react and then act to the problem. Whereas, the frontal brain thinker uses up precious time while attempting to explore all the options of the unknown. And while it is realized the analytical thought process may allow for a more accurate decision to be made, in a high risk/ time pressured event, the need for quick action and reaction takes precedence.

After all, this paradox of choice is not black and white, making it less scientific. The analytical type of decision making is always looking for the perfect decision that inevitably may never come-thus somewhat disproving Boyd's famous OODA Loop (Observe, Orient, Decide, and Act). Whereas, the instinctual reaction is merely looking for the best option at the time. In a society that demands perfection out of its law enforcement officers, the speed-accuracy tradeoff can have serious consequences, in-turn adding to the stress and over-analyzation of every decision. This is not to say that cops cannot utilize both the analytical and intuitional decision-making styles throughout one incident. Much like how we are taught to have cover and contact officers, our brain can balance the two styles so as to get us through something. For example, there may be a lull in a standoff with a subject trying to commit suicide by cop. Chances are we are all going to take our time and think through all of our options (analytical). However, the subject quickly disappears and flanks the officers unbeknownst to them and reappears nearby with a gun pointed right at the officers. Clearly, the Officers do not have time to explore all their options at this point, and they react by shooting him to protect themselves. This is just a very general example of how we can apply both decision making styles to an incident without even really realizing it.

Where we get into trouble is when we try to apply one style over the other when it does not exactly fit the situation. More often than not, we attempt to over-think a situation and allow for valuable time and real estate to be sucked-up.

With the make-up of the modern police force changing as more millennials fill the ranks, it is the hope of this research to show the importance of developing the intuition in these young people that may have strayed away from thousands of years of evolution that developed those survival instincts. Though it is through no fault of their own, as society has become more civilized, there is not as much need for humans to be on the alert and have quick reactions times to threats. But, it is my opinion that it is more important now than ever before to train our cops the best we can both for the safety of the officers as well as the public. This starts with psychoeducation and mental skills training.

Although my research was exploratory in nature, a scientific experiment would have been able to actually quantify the pros and cons of the analytical versus intuitional decision-making, as well as the speed versus accuracy trade-off between the two styles. As stated earlier, such research is going to take an abundance of time and technology to outfit a large sample of police officers with enough data collecting devices to truly come up with true to life data. Lab settings can come close to illustrating response times and heart rates, but nothing can compare to real life high risk stress. There has been 3D and virtual reality training tools designed specifically for law enforcement, however they still lack the realness of an actual life or death threat on the street (Parlow, 2017).

Furthermore, much of the research prior to this has assumed that all healthy brains are the same, however this research has illustrated that most people have a dominant hemisphere that is grossly influential on their decision making process; along with other variables such as gender, age, experience and past trauma.

Future Research

This book hopefully will spark future research in how analytical and intuitional minds influence decision making under stress, not only for police officers, but athletes and business people alike. Perhaps we will discover there is a deeper nexus to how people process information through their vision (ventral/dorsal) and how that may affect their decisions (Gilbert & Li, 2013). Also, researchers may be able to delve into the connection between Millennials and a lack of innate motor programming stemming from a lack of sports as youths. All in all, it is apparent researchers are just scratching the surface in the field of neuroscience. It is the hope of this book to possibly bridge the gap between academia and law enforcement so both can learn and benefit from one another. It has been confirmed via prior research and literature that there is a clear difference between the brain hemispheres. Most healthy humans utilize attributes of all parts, but there is a growing opinion in the field of neuroscience that most people have a dominant hemisphere that causes them to make decisions either more deliberately or dynamically. Furthermore, as the literature has shown, the deliberate decision making process is slower, which can be dangerous in the context of law enforcement decisions. But analytical brainers can learn to make more rapid decisions through training and experience so as to make their decisions more intuitional, which was shown to be faster and most often more accurate.

It is the goal of this research to provide a base to which future law enforcement instructors and administrators can base their opinions and also perhaps keep police officers safer in the face of ever-increasing danger.

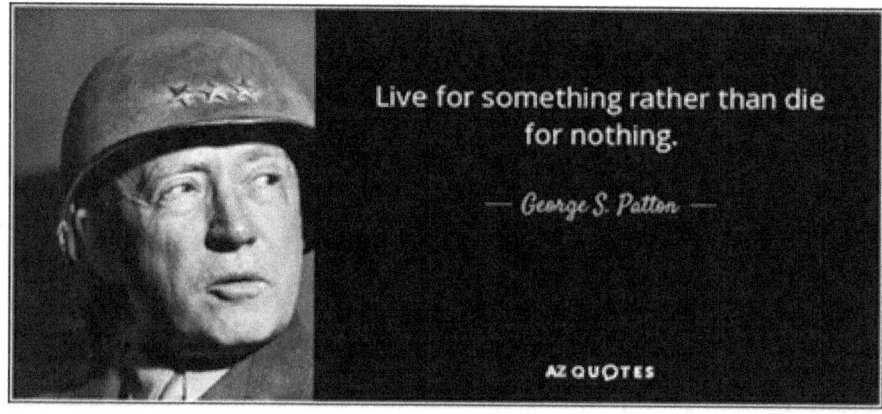

Chapter 3
COP VISION

"Lead me, follow me, or get out of my way."
                                        -Patton

As mentioned previously, I never realized how good my eyesight was until I started having millennial trainees in my car. Holy crap, they are all blind! My theory behind this is the fact that they grew up staring at TV and computer screens; the other possibility was that their mothers stopped breast feeding in the 80's and used formula instead which did not allow for the correct nutrients for their eyes to fully develop, but who really knows for certain. In any case, eyesight is where the rubber meets the road with regard to neuroscience, motor-programming and rapid decision-making. After all, if we cannot see, we cannot act. I have seen this come into play with trainees when they are developing probable cause (PC) to stop a suspect and also when they are simply contacting crooks. The typical modern trainee struggles to see the PC to make a stop because they cannot see the license plate numbers, or the furtive hand movements when suspects dump something. I have seen many trainees squinting and leaning forward in an attempt to see license plate numbers while we are stopped behind a car at a traffic light. And, yes, this is with contacts on. So if they are struggling to see plates at a dead stop, one can only imagine the avalanche of issues that happen when a situation or call turns violent or highly dynamic. See, none of the right brain/left brain, analytical vs. intuitional, speed vs. accuracy stuff works without vision! Thus, if we do not see the stimulus our brain cannot process it, and therefore our decision-making speed is going to be slower. And unfortunately, even if we teach our recruits what to look at intuitionally, there is still a void in terms of them having the inherent capability of actually seeing the stimulus in the first place. With society becoming more and more technologically dependent, I do not see this issue going away either. The more babies I see holding cell phones to their faces in restaurants as a modern pacifier, tells me the future of law enforcement is coming in blind in more ways than one.

Besides mandating Lasik surgery for such recruits, there is one way we can combat the issue of vision that would benefit all cops with good eyesight or not. The concept stemmed out of sports psychology and undoubtedly has a home in training police athletes. "Quiet Eye Training," has been used by Olympians and elite athletes for years and can be applied not only in firearms training, but on nearly every call for service. The technical definition of quiet eye, "is a fixation or tracking gaze that is located on a specific location or object in the visuomotor workspace within three degrees of visual angle for a minimum of 100 ms (Vickers, 2007)." To break down all that scientific mumbo jumbo, it is our eye's ability to stare at something without distraction, internally or externally. Furthermore, note the significance of the timeframe of 100 ms and how that corresponds with the 300 ms of reaction time mentioned in the previous chapters. The quiet eye is therefore a perception-action variable, in that it's onset is dictated by the onset of a specific movement in the task (2007). Think about when we are on the range and the instructor wants us to hit the bullseye or a certain part of the target from about 5 yards away.

In theory if we stare at that point prior to drawing and shooting, our eyes should link up to our motor programming and the barrel should be pointed right on target.

However, much like when a baseball player looks away in the process of swinging at a pitch, the shooter can take their eye off the intended target in the process of drawing or looking at their sights. This is where quiet eye training would benefit the police athlete in that they are able to focus throughout the process of a tactical task and follow-through. But much like anything else, if the shooter has never developed their eye speed and focus, it takes time to capitalize on such concepts. It is difficult for me to imagine a life without some sort of visual processing happening throughout my day. I grew up looking for deer and other wildlife on the side of the road. My dad taught me by example to always be scanning my environment, whether we were hunting or not. With that said, I reiterate that hunting is the number one way to develop vision in anyone, young or old, but especially in young people.

Even as outdoorsmen, we simply enjoy looking at wildlife and I grew up spotting stuff left and right. In retrospect, this helped me develop my vision and my ability to scan my environment nearly subconsciously. Secondly, I am a firm believer in sports and think this is another great way for children to develop eye speed and processing. To this day, I still spot deer and turkeys in the fields next to the freeway as I am driving to and from work. Sure it helps that I know what to look for, but I also believe over thirty years of visually processing my environment is great experience. When I am riding shotgun as an FTO, I often can tell trainees are not looking out past their headlights. Perhaps they miss an obvious vehicle code violation or a suspicious movement by a perp. If I notice this, I will have them do what is known by EVOC Instructors as, "horizon driving."

Essentially, in order for the driver to develop their skills in scanning their horizon, they will drive normally down the road and call out objects on both sides of the roadway such as a mailbox or speed limit sign. With practice, this will allow them to see how they were driving in a tunnel before and the importance of scanning way out in front of them, not only to catch bad guys but also for any possible hazards entering the street like a child riding a bicycle. Again, going back to reaction time and movement time, even if we see the hazard, our mind must react to it and our foot must hit the brakes in time so as to avoid a collision. So it is imperative we see the hazard sooner, so we have time to react and scanning can assist in this head start.

Side note: For those readers who have liberal cop hating friends, I often use this example so they can better understand reaction times. Since they will never understand the application of force, anyone who has driven a car has experienced a near collision or actual collision. I have them recall the incident and I point out the tunnel vision, rapid heart rate, shakiness, auditory exclusion and slow reaction times. When I illustrate these are all natural responses to fear, I attempt to have them imagine those same feelings and now they have to try to shoot a gun accurately at the same exact moment another car is crashing into them. When I explain to them this is much like an officer involved shooting, but without the legal decision-making process, I usually get some head nods. However if they still do not get it, I offer them a trip to the local gun range. There I will have them shoot a handgun at a point on the target. When they miss it repeatedly and their target looks like Swiss cheese, I point out that the liberal belief that we can shoot the knife out of someone's hand or shoot them in the foot is not feasible or safe. This has worked in the past and recommend it to anyone trying to educate a cop-hater.

Sorry I got off on a tangent, but it was an important point. I believe a lot of the "bad," decisions the media dislikes can be prevented with better vision. We can all make better decisions if we see and process stimulus sooner/better. This may seem like an obvious statement, but we continue to hire blind cops. Think about it this way, there is a reason the military will not allow blind servicemen to fly million dollar jets. Why should it be any different for cops that can cause a million dollar lawsuit?

Approximately 80 percent of all sensory information to the brain comes through the eyes (Teig, 2015). This is a considerable amount of info processing, so one can see how our vision can greatly affect not only what we see, but how our bodies react to that particular stimulus. Fluctuation of clarity can affect timing, depth perception, object detail variation, and other countless variations of vision. Thus, it is important to have a visual system that is flexible enough to adjust rapidly and guide the body's motor responses quickly and accurately so as to face the many changes in the surrounding environment. Any deficits in this system can slow the response of a police athlete, as well as make the responses unpredictable and inconsistent (2015). And it is not my intention to make excuses for others, but perhaps this last concept can shed some light on cases where Officers made mistakes of facts, such as mistaking a cell phone for a gun.

After all, our whole justification for use of force is built on the reasonable officer standard in Graham V. Connor. However, very seldom do critics take into consideration a "like officer vision," standard. Now I realize this could be skewed the other way too, and defense attorneys could argue cops cannot see furtive movements when suspects dump dope either for example.

But my point is not to give fodder for either side, rather to point out that many of our decisions start with our vision, whether good or bad. So instead of Officers being viewed as liars when they state they did not see something, perhaps there is an all too scary truth to their statements. The flow of information is typically broken down into three primary stages involving perceptual processes, decision-making and response selection/execution (Vickers, 2007).

It should be noted the first step in this process is perception. So the execution or end product is all based on what is believed to have been seen. One thing of importance to mention here is an example of "priming," which is the nonconscious form of human memory concerned with perceptual identification of words and objects. It refers to activating particular representations or associations in memory just before carrying out an action or task. For example, a person who sees the word "yellow" will be slightly faster to recognize the word "banana." This happens because yellow and banana are closely associated in memory. Additionally, priming can also refer to a technique in psychology used to train a person's memory in both positive and negative ways (Psychology Today, 2017).

For another law enforcement example of priming, I recall the officer involved shooting in 2009 where BART Officer Johannes Mehserle shot Oscar Grant. Without getting into the politics of the shooting, I will point out that Mehserle was involved in an arrest just the night before the incident, where they fought with an uncooperative subject that was found to have a gun in his waistband. Moreover, Oscar Grant's behavior mirrored that of the armed subject, so Mehserle was primed to think Grant was armed just like the other arrest (pattern recognition).

Again, this is the reason when an officer is involved in a critical incident, the detectives and district attorney investigators ask the shooter if they were recently involved in any violent calls or calls that did not sit well with them, such as a suicide by cop call. In a way priming can blur our vision and make the perception that much heavier, in-turn playing a vital role in the response.

More time is needed when the information is complex, when we are in a novel situation, or when we have not yet learned to attend to what is most important in the environment (Vickers, 2007). Sounds more like a summation of field training huh? This concept of visual attention is important because even if a trainee does not have the best eyesight, perhaps we can still train them what to look at, which would assist in the overall processing speed.

The "binding problem," concerns our capacity to integrate information across time, space, attributes and ideas (2007). Anyone who has learned 15 different twist locks, wrist locks and take-downs in defensive tactics has fallen victim to this human dilemma where we cross-wire the techniques, especially under stress. One way to overcome the binding problem is "chunking" (2007). Through training and experience, one can learn to chunk the concepts or ideas together in fewer pieces of information. Not only is this great for learning, but chunking can help the trainee to rapidly process what is important so they do not have to continually return what is not as important to their safety and overall handling of a call. Such gaze control can be focused on fixed and moving targets. However the problem for both the attentional system and gaze is to focus on the most critical part of the target and time the acquisition of information so that there is an optimal "coupling," between the gaze and the aiming movements (2007).

Anyone who has tried to hit a golf ball without looking down felt the lack of such coupling. As the number of visuomotor workspaces increase, a cognitive decision has to be made as to what field is the most important to attend to, or else panic will set in, ultimately affecting performance. As eluded to earlier, this scanning of one's environment is something the Millennial struggles with, so they must learn the visual pivot early on in their training.

I will address a variety of training techniques in the training chapter of this book, however this chapter clearly illustrated the importance of cop vision. The sports world is clearly light years ahead of law enforcement in terms of quiet eye training and performance psychology, however I hope this book will show the need for updated training in our profession. I hate to admit it, but if we want to be treated like professionals, we must train like professionals. This means constantly sharpening our skills and becoming more aware of our weaknesses, such as vision.

Chapter 4
PSYCHOEDUCATION AND MENTAL SKILLS TRAINING

"By perseverance, study, and eternal desire, any man can become great."

-Patton

In the article, "Brief Mental Skills Training Improves Memory and Performance in High Stress Police Cadet Training, (2016)," the authors found through empirical evidence how psychological performance training, such as breathing techniques, mental imagery and attentional focus, has reduced stress in police cadets. Which in-turn aids in cognitive processing, better memory recall, arousal control and greater overall confidence; thus resulting in better decision-making, which is truly the ultimate goal of training (Page, Asken, Zwemer, & Guido, 2016). Concentration, awareness and guided visualization are the three components that can separate the expert from the novice. Thus part of becoming a peak performer entails self-mastery. This is done by constantly cultivating the *mind-body system*. As law enforcement professionals, we have to do it better and faster than ever before, and it starts with self-education. As author Stephen M.R. Covey once said, "Seek first to understand and then to be understood" (Divine, 2015).

To tie in with the previous article, "Positive Effects of Imagery on Police Officers' Shooting Performance under Threat (2014)," explores the many benefits of mental skills training for police officers, but delves deeper in namely mental imagery. Although the authors are from the Netherlands, their research of Human Movement Sciences is still applicable to American Law Enforcement.

The most important takeaway from the article was that mental imagery strengthens the neural pathways needed to perform the action in real life. Moreover, mental imagery can assist in quickly developing a trainee's intuitional decision-making because they have already done the action so many times in their mind's eye. Also another bi-product would be increased confidence and decreased anxiety, which is always a plus in any performance domain, especially for Millennials who may be lacking confidence (Colin, Nieuwenhuys, Visser, & Oudejans, 2014). This point is further illustrated in the nexus between the "high-risk," professions with high intensity sports, such as those that entail physical contact. The police athlete must battle injuries, recovery and self-assessment, just like a regular athlete so "Psychological Skills Training (PST)," can benefit those in police work as well (Birrer & Morgan, 2010).

Another take on police performance was explored to address the many benefits to mental skills training for law enforcement officers which also reveals how mental imagery can prevent the maladaptive responses to stress and trauma (Arble, Lumley, Pole, Blessman, & Arnetz, 2017).This *self-care* is another important part of the performance of police officers. In essence, by conducting preventative mental skills coaching, officers are more likely to accept it, versus addressing a mental "problem," after the fact (2017). Moreover, those in a bravado type environment like law enforcement are less likely to reach out or accept help, so buy-in to mental skills training must happen early on in their career so as to take full advantage of the process.

For those of us that have been FTO's, force options instructors or have taught at the academy, we all realize that there is a huge disconnect between what is taught in the academy and what really happens on the street. Clearly this gap is probably much larger in the more ghetto jurisdictions, however I believe this wedge is only going to become larger as the standards continue to fall. By now I have brow beaten my readers about the Pussification of law enforcement, and the academies are not immune to such scrutiny. The question administrators and instructors alike must ask themselves is; are we truly training these recruits to be ready for a fight for their lives their first day on the job? The answer is no, hell no. As mentioned before, many of these people have never played sports or done anything athletic, so they never developed the mental toughness needed to power through the mental and physical stressors of the job. Moreover, because the academies are getting soft, the recruits are still not becoming inoculated to such stress. The academies used to weed out the weaklings so they would not even make it to the streets, now the academies push out lemons like a Ford manufacturing plant. With that said, if we are going to continue down this path, we might as well give them some tools needed to not only survive but win the fight. After all, like I tell my trainees, we can all survive in a hospital bed, I want to _win._

This is where my second Master's degree comes in. I took an interest in a relatively up and coming degree program known as Performance Psychology. This field evolved out of Sport Psychology and the techniques used are well known to many Olympians, professional ball players and athletes alike. However performance psychology encompasses the much larger domain of not only athletes but any person who must perform at their peak, such as businessmen, soldiers and cops. Hence, I jumped into the field; curious to see how I could apply it to the streets.

I quickly decided that police athletes have a great need to learn the many mental techniques in performance psychology and it all starts in the academies. For it is evident there is an even larger void in all of law enforcement that bridges the gap between the physical and mental training. Sure we learn all the wrist locks and twist locks, but what happens when everything goes to shit and that rookie has to fight through the stress, quandary and pain involved in a street fight?

Sadly, we see the results of this question all too often on the evening news. Panic sets in because Officers are not afforded the mental or physical tools to overcome resistance and effect force with confidence. Obviously confidence is built upon a foundation of training and experience, but what I suggest is that if we first work on what is going on between their ears, then Officers will be more apt in applying the physical skills. For example, how often do we see a young officer begin to struggle on FTO or at the range, and they cannot recover from their downward spiral because their confidence is shot?

But as agencies we do not focus on their mental game, we keep doing what cops do best; point of the weaknesses and tell them everything they are fucking up. Great confidence builder right? If they start learning the mental game in the academy, perhaps they can learn to recover rather than sink. Choose any famous ball player, and I can show you an athlete that had the skills to be successful but had to overcome their biggest opponent to truly win. That opponent is in their mind.

One of the most common terms in Performance Psychology is negative self-talk. Essentially, negative self-talk is the internal dialogue we all have with ourselves that negatively effects our performance.

We are all guilty of it and I am sure every reader can think of a time when this really hit home. The next time you are watching a ball game on T.V., and watch the players after they miss a free throw or go out on strikes swinging. The head shake and look of disappointment tells me all I need to know about their internal dialogue. They are already mind-fucking themselves so bad that it is showing up in a subconscious movement- and these are the professionals! So imagine what the little rookie who has never been outside the city limits, let alone dialed an outside area code on a land-line, is going to handle a street brawl where some thug is trying to take his gun. I can bet money the self-talk going on in that little mind is not, "I'm gonna fucking kill this asshole, he ain't getting my gun, dominate!" No, I imagine the untrained mind is more like, "Oh shit, please don't kill me, man this guy is strong, Mommy, help!" Obviously this is an extreme case, but one can get the picture how positive versus negative self-talk can be the difference between success and failure or life and death. But my guess is most readers have never heard of negative self-talk, even though I am sure they have fallen victim to it. My belief is often times when we can put a label on something, it is then easier to identify and overcome. In the case of negative self-talk, now that we know what it is, I think the rookie in the academy, all the way to the Chief of Police can benefit.

So how do you overcome negative self-talk once you identify it you ask? Well, unfortunately this feat is often easier said than done, but to simplify the question; have positive self-talk! Much like that Seinfeld episode where George decided to do the complete opposite of whatever he ever thought and it worked for him. As performers we must learn to disrupt the negative internal dialogue and replace it with positive thoughts.

For those Coppers out there that get nervous on the range before qualification, not giving into the negative self-talk is paramount. Instead of thinking, "Oh fuck I'm gonna fail, I know it," let's think something like, "I got this, I've qualified before." Such positive self-talk will not only eliminate the powerful line of negative self-talk but also build confidence at the same time. Thus every bullet will not be stressed over and failing will not become a self-fulfilling prophecy.

This reminds of a story I heard during my studies that stuck with me and can truly illustrate the great power our minds have over matter: Picture an older gentleman in the early 1900's who worked at a railroad company. His job was to look after the refrigerated railroad cars. One day the man was checking on the last railroad car and the door shut on him. He was the last one at the depot and he knew it. He panicked and cried for help but no one came. The man began to carve in the ice walls that he loved his wife and children and believed he would not survive a night in the freezing box car. When they found him the next day, he indeed was dead, however the refrigerated box car was not plugged in. Rather the interior of the box car was only a mere 50 degrees and he easily could have survived. However, the internal dialogue he had with himself only prepared him for death. That man allowed his mind to talk himself into dying in a survivable situation.

And I hate to second guess any of my fallen comrades that have died in the line of duty, but I also hate to think how many of them allowed this same thing to happen to them.
The mind is an incredibly powerful tool, and I think through no fault of their own, most knuckle dragging cops only use a fraction of it.

Another common tool in the Performance Psychology bat belt, is visualization. This is essentially the mental act of picturing ourselves going through a set of motions so as to complete a skill. I have had great luck using this technique for trainees who were suffering with not "going by the numbers," on traffic stops. For example, if a trainee continues to forget to turn on his spotlight or struggles with the radio traffic, I will have them park in the lot of PD (because it is safe), and sit in the driver's seat quietly. On their own, I will ask them to walk themselves through what they think a "routine," traffic stop should look like with their eyes closed, to include: picking up the radio, talking on the radio, activating the emergency lights and siren, turning on the spotlight, parking the vehicle and exiting. Now this may sound like some hippie bullshit but it works. Without getting too technical, basically the mind will burn the same neurons needed to complete the task in reality. So that way when the trainee actually does it in person, their mind already has seen the steps before and they are not completely foreign; thus easier to remember.

Moreover, much like with positive self-talk, if we see ourselves succeeding in our mind's eye, it will subconsciously build our self-confidence. It has been said, even imaging ourselves to be more like a confident individual that we admire can help boost our confidence. This is truly a real life example of monkey see monkey do. Be forewarned that visualization will not work if the trainee is not fully committed to the technique. Also, the environment must be free of any distractions, so perhaps the trainee might have to do it at home before bed.

In any case, visualization can be a very valuable tool if used correctly and is another widely known technique, I am just putting a title to it.

The next mental skills technique I would like to explore is self-evaluation or self-analysis. This tool is commonly used by athletes so as to identify both their strengths and weaknesses, along with learning to quickly adapt and change them so as to improve and overcome adversity. An example would be a baseball player who repeatedly looks towards third base as he swings for the fences, inevitably missing the ball coming across the plate. A true athlete will recognize when this movement is occurring and fix the mistake so as to have better hand-eye contact with the bat to the ball. Another law enforcement related example would be a cop who continually jerks the trigger on the range, causing his shots to go all over his target. Being the professional he is, the shooter realizes this movement and changes his trigger squeeze to be nice and smooth to the rear.

Regardless of the skill, performers must first learn what is right and then they can in-turn feel what is right. We should constantly be self-evaluating ourselves on several levels. A true professional should be open to new ideas and never stop sharpening the tip of the spear. We are forever students of our profession and should be able to self-diagnose at any given moment, whether it be on the range, on the mat or in the streets. To that end, positive self-talk, mental imagery, and self-evaluation can all be utilized in the next performance psychology technique, which is goal-setting.

The key to remembering goal-setting is the acronym S.M.A.R.T. Goals should be, Specific, Measurable, Adjustable, Realistic, and Time Referenced (2017). This may sound simple, but ask a millennial just how many goals he/she has set in their life and the answer may come as a surprise. Again, recall the contemporary rookie who has played little or no sports, and has little ambition in their life. As a result, goal-setting may be a relatively new and foreign concept for most. So perhaps short-term and long-term goals must be laid out. Such goals may include getting hired by an agency, completing Field Training, or passing probation. These are pretty general and larger goals. However, larger goals can be overwhelming and add more stress to someone. In order for goals to work, we must start small and as these smaller goals are achieved, it in-turn boosts confidence. If we look at trying to eat an entire elephant with a fork and knife in one sitting, it appears to be impossible. However, if we break those bites up over the course of a career, then the achievement ain't as cumbersome. The way I explain it to my trainees is, *little wins*. A bunch of little wins will amount to be a big win in the long run.

Not to sound cliché, but we all can benefit by taking one step at a time and checking off many small goals, rather than a few big goals. In fact, every cop should write a set of goals for his career and come back to them every once in a while to update them. So many coppers get stuck in a rut and simply countdown to retirement without breaking down those remaining years with short term and long term goals. For the trainee, they might want to set a goal of mastering the aforementioned traffic stop. They can utilize all the mental skills training and once they hit that mark, move on to another goal. All the while this will only build their confidence and assist them getting through whatever the street throws at them.

Think about how hard it is to go for a jog with no destination or time measure in mind. It is much easier and motivating to set a goal of two miles in fifteen minutes. As cops it is difficult to become goal-orientated because our mission is not always clear. Sure traffic cops want to get tickets and detectives want to clear homicides, but what is the patrolman's goal? I always had supervisors tell me that I need to be "well-rounded," meaning an equal amount of cites, F.I.'s, cases and arrests. What the fuck kind of goal is that? Talk about a goal being too general! Perhaps one day police administrators will take a hard look at what the back bone of their agencies goals are and make more mission orientated cops, like in the military. Until then, it is up to us to teach our young people to set goals and motivate our elders to do the same.

After all, places like Google and Apple did not get to where they are today by sticking with the status quo and telling their employees to be "well-rounded." Just perhaps law enforcement will step away from the cancerous, "That's the way it's always been," attitude and step foot in the 21st century.

We can have all the technology in the world, but if we do not have smart motivated cops, what do we truly have? To illustrate my point, after finishing up my degree I was talking to one of the rookies who wanted to be a K9 handler. He was one of those guys that got into this later in life so he was not the typical hard-charging young guy straight out of the academy. I pulled him aside and asked him what his short term and long term goals were as it pertained to getting a dog. When he did not really have an answer, I knew I was onto something. I explained to him he needed to prove himself and generate some cases, get into some shit if you will.

I advised him to set a short term goal of getting a pro-active arrest every day. Then maybe a long-term goal could be getting a certain number of stolen cars or guns. He seemed receptive and admitted to me given the political nature in law enforcement, it is easy to drive past that "good stop." However, he believed the goal setting system would help him stay motivated to remain pro-active.

Another way to stay motivated and on-track with one's goals, is to develop your "why." Why did we become cops in the first place? Why do we want to be a great trainer? K9 Handler? Supervisor? When we have something larger to buy into, something larger than ourselves, it is easier to make decisions because everything goes back to that why. I personally developed a mantra for myself and use it both in self-talk and when I say goodbye to one of my fellow brothers. Instead of saying the typical cop, "stay safe," I started to think that was somewhat redundant.

Of course, we are going to stay safe, even a coward can stay safe. My personal mantra evolved out of my why, which is to be the best Force Options Instructor I could possibly be, because if I could be influential in never losing another fellow cop, by God I was going to do it. And I firmly believe my calling is to keep other cops safe. Thus, before I hit a door I tell myself, "Stay dangerous." When I part ways from another cop, I tell them, "Stay dangerous." This is a constant reminder that we are in a dangerous world that requires us to be more dangerous than the wolves of society. Staying dangerous means we mustn't become complacent both mentally and physically. Many athletes have a saying they tell themselves when the stress is thick and there is no reason cops can't do the same.

When I tell myself to stay dangerous, it means I have to continually sharpen the spear, so not to become more like the wood of the spear. To those that argue this is the wrong mindset to have, I point to the coward in Florida who failed to save the young children being killed by an active shooter. A personal mantra can again provide a peak performer with a code to live by and can be another tool to add to the overall mental toughness needed to overcome resistance when that terrible day comes.

Training guru Tony Blauer teaches us about the "three fights." The first being inside our own minds. This is often the biggest fight because it is based on our confidence in our skills, power and ability to fight and win. The second fight is the actual altercation. And the third fight is the fight against the system. Having been sued, this is a whole new kind of fight, and often times can be the most stressful. So from a performance psych standpoint there are a few take-aways from this concept. The first being, we must obviously be confident in ourselves. And I do not mean like the two year rookie, who's so cocky he can't fit his head in the door. Rather, I mean actually confident before, during and after a fight. Having confidence before will cut down on the fear and anxiety of an altercation. Confidence during the fight will allow for clear thinking and less panic. And lastly, confidence in ourselves in that fight against the system will lower the stress and allow us to articulate ourselves in a more educated/ professional manner.

Another concept brought forth in an article written in the Journal of Cyber Therapy and Rehabilitation that I took great interest in was the preventative stress-inoculation training being conducted for our soldiers prior to being deployed. The article was titled, "Pre-deployment stress inoculation training for primary prevention of combat-related stress disorders." Author Horani stated, "The conceptual basis for using SIT as a preventive approach against developing stress-related symptoms after exposure to trauma is based on studies which have shown that enhanced stress-resilience is associated with a protective physiologic stress response. Specifically, a reduction of anxiety within 72 hours of exposure to a traumatic event is associated with lower risk of PTSD or greater effectiveness of debriefing (2011)." I hope to one day pre-emptively provide this same training utilizing the same concepts learned here for our nation's police officers so as to prevent further psychological casualties.

Stress Inoculation Training (SIT) can be defined as a combination of information giving, Socratic discovery-orientated inquiry, cognitive restructuring, problem solving, relaxation training, behavioral rehearsals, self-monitoring, self-instruction, self-reinforcement, and modifying environmental situations (Meichenbaum, 2008). Again, these techniques coincide with the mental skills training utilized in Sport and Performance Psychology, to include: breathing control, positive self-talk and naturally psychoeducation.

Athletes have been using all of these techniques for years, but law enforcement is really behind on the times. Most of these terms the reader can probably guess what they entail, while others may need to be looked up.

In any event, cops can train themselves or ideally these techniques can be implemented into the POST curriculum; to be taught at the academies and in advanced officer training. This way they will be properly instructed and become a standard within the field. But this process will not happen over-night and I understand positive psychology techniques are easier said than done.

Anyone who watches any professional sport can see how confidence can come and go for even the most elite athletes. Thus without the negatives in life, we would not have positives right? Furthermore, it is very natural for us to be negative. Throughout history for survival's sake, our rational brain is bias towards the negative. It must decide and act on life-threatening influences daily, and has been conditioned to be pessimistic and scared a result of the steady diet of negatives (Divine, 2015). So cops, who go in and out of survival mode daily become even more cynical than the average Joe Schmoe.

Lastly, breathing is free medicine. This might be the most important concept in our whole performance psychology bat-belt. It has been called tactical breathing, box-breathing, combat breathing, whatever the name, the point is just fucking breathe. We have all had that feeling of pressure moving up our body towards our throat and a tightness in our chest as a result of anxiety. In cases where there is time pressure, ideally taking at least one deep breath subconsciously is ideal. But until that level of training comes, remember to simply breathe in through the nose and out the mouth until that pressure subsides.

I have been getting ready to kick a door or driving in vehicles pursuits and two deep breaths calmed me right down so I could handle business. The benefits are huge and there are some other bi-products to breath control that some may not be aware of. The first one is the importance of getting fresh oxygen to our brains so we can make clear cognitive decisions. Secondly, if we are in the middle of a fight, breathing will allow the police athlete to not tire as quickly. We have all seen the academy recruit hit the bag with a baton and forget to breathe or give commands. Pretty quickly they are gassed and gasping for air because they were holding their breath while delivering blows. So in short, I do not care what "tactical," name you give it, just breathe one or two big breaths, and I think you will be surprised by the results.

As I have said before, it all starts in the academies. The curriculum must change. By adding performance psychology to the learning domains, recruits can hit the street with more confidence. That confidence will make them not only safer but smarter. Safe and smart cops will end up on YouTube much less and go home to their families at the end of the night. Once the academies get on board, agency orientation and field training will allow for the trainee to apply their mental skills in a practical environment. Following that, officers will continue to use their mental skills throughout their careers. I am sure many of the readers are thinking they would have liked to have had some performance psychology training a long time ago before they made all those dumb mistakes and developed other coping methods to deal with them. After all, it is never too late to try.

In California we have the Peace Officer Standards & Training Commission (POST). I am sure most other states have a similar governing body to oversee local police agencies. In any case, I believe POST does a decent job, however much like with the absence of performance psychology techniques in training, I believe the way we go about training is seriously outdated. Modern educators are constantly developing new ways that students learn and comprehend. But most law enforcement agencies are still using antiquated teaching techniques and are limiting how much our cops retain. For example, as instructors, we attempt to jam as much as we can into an 8 or 10 hour training day. In the academy and in-service training, block learning is usually the presentation of choice. Block style learning is useful for teaching new techniques because the learner can learn each technique or concept step-by-step. Quick results sure, but studies have found this does little or nothing for instilling the information in the trainees long-term memory.

Think about when we are taught ten different wrist locks, twist locks and arm-bars. The trainee learns the technique in their short-term memory, but has to be re-taught the techniques on the following defensive tactics day, 6 months later. This tells me two things: 1) They clearly did not retain the techniques, 2) They clearly are not using the techniques on the street correctly, if not at all. So how do we combat this?

Interleaving education needs to be implemented by POST, especially in the academies. This style of teaching essentially is the complete opposite of block training in that it is far more sporadic. The concept behind it is basically to make the learner recall what they learned at different times, further cementing the material in their long-term memory.

For example, after teaching an arm-bar, the student is then taught something totally different like hand-cuffing. But then is forced to show the prior arm-bar or even demonstrate it in a scenario later in the day. The process is repeated throughout the day, week, or months so as to keep exposing the learner as well as make them apply it correctly to the context. After all, it is applying the proper technique in the proper context that should be our end goal. With that said, I believe it is time to eliminate some of the antiquated defensive tactics techniques and firearms qualifications to better prepare the trainees for real-life situations. The truth is they are not going to remember 20 different twist locks and escapes and they are not going to ever use their off-hand supported shooting position from 25 yards or more. We are only as good as our training and we are failing miserably at providing our cops with the best possible training that is both contemporary and forward-thinking.

If everyone is
thinking alike,
then somebody
isn't thinking.

George S. Patton

Chapter 5
SELF-CARE

"You're never beaten until you admit it."

-Patton

Speaking of stupid mistakes, I cannot go on without mentioning sleep. Yes, that evil thing we cops rarely get. This habit is slowly killing us and it is difficult to follow through on any goal or have positive self-talk if we are tired. I know the old salts are saying, "No shit," right about now, but hear me out. In line with agencies stepping into the 21st century, it is evident that lack of sleep is an unseen epidemic in law enforcement across the nation. I look forward to the day agencies figure out that sleep is the number one reason we fuck up and cost them money. Most departments have policies in place for the amount of hours we can work, but what about amount of sleep we get? Agency leaders turn their head when a graveyard cop works all night and sits in court all day, just to return to work that night. This is the same cop that is expected to make life or death decisions with perfection, oh and not to mention drive around in a 3200 pound bullet. One day it is going to come out that lack of sleep is our #1 issue and is detrimental to our safety both on and off the streets. There is a reason cops die an average of 18 years sooner than the rest of the population. Lack of sleep, shiftwork and cortisol are at the top of the list. The health problems that stem from lack of sleep, like diabetes and heart disease, are only the tip of the iceberg. So what are agencies doing to take care of their people?

We all have heard that being up for 24 hours is comparative to being a .08 blood alcohol content, but unfortunately shiftwork on a cop's schedule is not that easy of equation. Having worked graveyards for years, I know I cut my life short, and probably some relationships too. Many of days, my sleep would be broken, rather than sleeping 7 or 8 straight hours like a normal human being. On my Monday, sometimes I would go to bed around 0300 hrs., sleep for 3 hours, wake up hungry and get up to eat. Then I would lay in bed trying to fall asleep and when I finally did, I only would maybe get another hour or two of sleep. And then the worst part was having to be up for another few hours before even going to work. Once at work, I would pound caffeine- way over the daily dose amount to stay awake. But you guessed it, I have court at 0800 hrs. Since the DA's are silver spoon babies themselves, they do not understand how it is to work graveyards so they hold me hostage in court, just to not testify. Then I finally go home around 1200 hrs., just to wake up at 1800 hrs., and do it all over again. Sounds healthy right?

This is just the start of our demise, leading to a high divorce rate, interpersonal problems, cynicism, hypertension, stress, gastro intestinal problems, sleep disorders, burn out, and eventually heart attacks, just to name a few. Paradoxically, the same hypervigilance needed to survive on the streets is inevitably what kills the cops in the long run. Ultimately, by maintaining such a high level of performance for so long, the typical cop burns out and their performance is affected, closely followed by their health, both mental and physical.

Dr. Kevin Gilmartin, Ph.D., is a consultant for law enforcement and in his article titled, "Hypervigilance," he speaks to the effects to mental and physical health throughout the course of a law enforcement career. Gilmartin writes, "A perceptual set of being vigilant of events in one's environment leads to a state of being hypervigilant or over-reactive to potentially threatening situations. At a bio-behavioral level, it is the role of the reticular activating system to scan inputs from the perceptual field and determine which events should be interpreted as threatening and which as neutral (2006)." Unlike any other job, such 'hypervigilance' is imperative for not only on the job performance, but survival. Furthermore, a police officer cannot just turn this function on and off, so he/she develops an almost paranoid and exaggerated information processing habit that becomes second nature every day and every waking hour. Some simple steps that a police family may regard as normal may seem borderline schizophrenic to others, such as when a police officer sits in a restaurant, he must always sit with his back to the wall and ideally likes to see the entrance. This way he can see everyone coming into the restaurant, scan them, and act accordingly if a threat arises. But do not think this is a practice reserved only for when he is in uniform. No, the hypervigilant police officer will do this in and out of uniform, with or without his family and friends. Or else he will suffer from anxiety for the unknown going on behind him will eat at him so much he will be unable to concentrate on the conversation at the table and will probably be constantly looking around to ensure his safety. Sound healthy? Of course not, but this is just one example of a day in the life of a police officer.

Gilmartin goes on to say, "The feeling of energy, wit, and camaraderie will be correlated with the work place. As the officer arrives home, the hypervigilant perceptual set is held in abeyance in the safety of his/her own home. However, the pendulum of homeostasis swings into a parasympathetic state of tiredness, numbness, and an almost detached exhaustion when interacting with the less threatening and more mundane tasks of after work home-life. The hypervigilance and consequent "street-high" of the work place leads to the "off-duty depression" of the parasympathetic swing in an attempt to homeostatically revitalize the body (2006)." However, "off-duty," is still a gray area for most cops. The only other profession that becomes part of one's identity like being a police officer, is a doctor. No one introduces "Joe the garbage man," at the party as such, but police officer or 'cop' will almost always be latched onto a cop's name whether he is on or off duty. So being 'off-duty,' is somewhat of a misnomer. Cops are never truly off-duty and are held to a higher standard both on and off the clock. Furthermore, most cops carry a gun off-duty for the possibility of running into one of their prior arrests or disgruntled 'clients,' so even the tools to which they wear on their body force them to remain in constant heightened level of alertness.

One can see how the job can quickly start to deteriorate a cop's interpersonal relationships and how his performance on the job effects everything else around him, mirroring many traits or impairments of a psychological disorder. The American Psychiatric Association states that a mental disorder, "is associated with present distress (e.g., a painful symptom) or disability (i.e., impairment in one or more areas of functioning) or with significantly increased risk of suffering pain, death, disability, or an important loss of freedom (2012)."

Now one could argue that a police officer's behavior is not outright maladaptive, in fact he is acting within the norm of the police culture, and therefore, the behavior is not indicative of psychosis or a disorder. The other argument is that hypervigilance causes sustained distress, burnout, interpersonal issues, and health issues, so it most definitely falls into being a disorder.

Moreover, many of the traits that a police officer develops over time are consistent with many of the personality disorders, such as generalized anxiety disorder, acute stress disorder, narcissistic and antisocial personality disorder. This is not to imply every Officer out there is a crazed lunatic waiting to snap at any given moment, but perhaps if administrators are educated on the psychological tendencies, they can limit the mental and physical trauma of their people in the future.

'Burnout,' is the state of being overwhelmed by stress, and is usually experienced by highly motivated professionals faced with high work demands. More than ever before, police officers are under great pressure to perform flawlessly, all the while being short staffed and battling the age old stressors of such a high risk occupation. "People who feel burned out, lack energy, and are filled with frustration and tension. Emotional symptoms of burnout include a loss of interest in work, decreased work performance, feelings of helplessness, and trouble sleeping (Aamodt 2013)." Sleep disorders will be addressed in further detail later, but burnout can also cause cynicism towards others and the organization, which may eventually lead to absenteeism, a high turnover, or even depression (2013). So when we examine any organization, one could probably find a number of employees or athletes that fit this criteria. I would venture to say the percentage is even higher in any given law enforcement agency, especially the smaller ones because more of a work load is usually placed on each individual. Burnout clearly leads to many other side effects but it can be a tell-tale sign something is brewing inside those officers. But as each officer practices his/her hypervigilance both on and off duty, the likelihood of burnout steadily increases to the point where it is almost inevitable for each officer to go through it at one point in their career.

However, much like the police suicide rates, there is little data on the topic of burnout, for the tough police culture will always prevail.

Another cause for burnout is various shifts an officer works. Obviously being awake throughout the night is not normal, so working nights inherently has its own set of problems that come along with it. It is estimated that shiftwork affects roughly 25% of employees, however, amongst law enforcement it is much higher (2013). Aside from the obvious physical problems such as chronic fatigue, increased risk for diabetes and gastrointestinal problems, the psychosocial effects are just as detrimental. Much time is spent alone because a cop who works nights is wide awake when mostly everyone else is asleep, including his family and friends.

In-turn, the night shift officer is only exposed to other cynical cops and suspects who in their eyes cannot be trusted, thus further separating him from the norms of society. This is why many officers begin to only socialize with other cops even off duty, because no one else understands their sleep patterns and their outlook on life; which as we are finding out is very much skewed.

However with that said, those who have never worked all night do have a difficult time imagining sleeping all day. A relatively new concept is an actual, 'shiftwork sleep disorder,' that involves problems with the body's 24 hour clock or circadian rhythms (2014). "Light and dark help the body know when to be active and when to rest. Light is a cue to be awake, while dark tells the body to sleep. When one works at night and sleep during the day, the body's internal clock needs to reset to let the body sleep during the day (2014)."

However, even with blackout blinds and sleeping pills, often times the body fights to sleep during the day. Couple the body's natural biological rejection to sleeping during the day, with family, neighbors and social events, and the result is a large number of officers going to work on little or no sleep.

From the National Institute of Justice (NIJ), "Continual breaks in circadian rhythm can cause serious mental and physical fatigue. This fatigue diminishes people's mental and physical health, and impairs their ability to deal with stressful situations. For police officers, this gives way to a cycle of fatigue that decreases their ability to perform their job effectively (2012)." The DSM-5 classifies sleep disorders as "Sleep-Wake Disorders." Insomnia Disorder is described as having difficulty initiating and maintaining sleep, plus early morning awakening with the inability to fall back asleep. Another disorder listed in the DSM-5, which is likely to affect most officers working the night shift, is the "Circadian Rhythm Sleep-Wake Disorder." This disorder even states that it is usually brought on by one's occupational schedule and is a persistent sleep disruption that causes excessive sleepiness, distress and impairment (2013). Which is contradictive to every police officer's goal of being safe and making rapid life or death decisions. The NIJ further illustrates this scary statistic, "Sleep deprivation is comparable to excessive drinking. A sleep deprivation study found that not sleeping for 17 hours impaired a person's motor skills to an extent equivalent to having an alcohol toxicity of 0.05 percent. Not sleeping for 24 hours was equivalent to a toxicity level of 0.08 percent. This level of deprivation would impair speech, balance, coordination and mental judgment (2009)."

Yet Officers across the nation continue to work overtime, double shifts and on average get half of the required sleep needed to function, but drive countless hours and perform at a high risk level in the middle of the night; making rapid, or sometimes not, decisions daily.

So how does one suppose Officers counter their sleep deprivation? Lots and lots of caffeine. As an article from Officer.com, titled, "The Growing Concern About Energy Drinks," puts it, "Caffeine, despite its long and nearly universal popularity, is still a psychoactive drug capable of creating both dependence and increasing tolerance in its users similar to alcohol and other drug users. Taken in excess caffeine can hurt us and, in extreme but not unheard of circumstances, may even lead to death, (2015)." To that end, coffee is slowly drifting in popularity amongst younger cops and the more potent energy drinks are becoming the drug of choice. Despite the growing knowledge on the risk of cardiac issues, headaches, sleep disorders, addiction, anxiety, diuretic effects, and even stimulant psychosis, cops still continue to guzzle away on energy drinks daily, even when they are off duty (2015). Why?

They must maintain that hypervigilance. As a result, cops fall yet again into another disorder listed in the DSM-5. "Caffeine Intoxication," is when a so-called high dose of caffeine (250 mg) is consumed. It should be noted that is also the same amount listed on commonly sold energy drinks. Five common symptoms such as restlessness, nervousness, excitement, insomnia and tachycardia qualify many cops as having a caffeine related disorder (2013).

But the need to maintain that 'high,' overrides any health risks for it is widely excepted in the police culture that being tired is just part of the job, so much so that a common phrase that is tossed around is, "You can sleep when you're dead." And dead is what is inevitable. Gilmartin found that the average life expectancy of a police officer compared to the rest of the population is 18 years less. Also, the average officer only lives roughly 5 years after retirement (2006). Many officers become so consumed with the job that their hobbies begin to fade and have nothing left after retirement. Sadly enough, many officers find that nothing like police work gives them that high and they have nothing else to live for.

As we explore the depths of police psychology and physiology, one scary truth is many police officers may be suffering from disorders or disorder-like symptoms and not even know it. "Acute Stress Disorder," is probably a disorder that may go on throughout a career untreated and may explain why many officers self-medicate via substance abuse. The Acute Stress Disorder mentions, "Experiencing repeated or extreme exposure to aversive details of traumatic events, 2013)." Depending on how busy the city or county a cop works in, exposure to trauma could be a daily occurrence. Furthermore, many officers fall into the 5 categories listed in the DSM-5, such as, intrusion symptoms, negative mood, dissociative symptoms, avoidance and arousal symptoms (2013).

To explain intrusion, many officers suffer from nightmares and sustained distress from prior calls that did not go as planned, or fears that their weapon will not work in the future. Also, many officers compartmentalize their feelings as a defense mechanism from seeing trauma. In-turn, often times they are unable to express their feelings or are able to turn their emotions off.

Again this is a trait that is expected in the police culture for mere self-protection. However, it takes a toll on the cop's personal interactions. Moreover, officers can become dissociative and avoiding after an event whether it be a memory gap as a result from stress, or a protective barrier in an attempt to shut out the trauma. Either way, this disconnection is rarely understood by outsiders and is far from societal 'normative' behavior. Lastly, arousal symptoms include sleep disturbances, irritable behavior and yes, hypervigilance (2013).

Another result of a cop's constant hypervigilance, caffeine consumption and inherent occupational pressures, many also fall victim to "Generalized Anxiety Disorder." Some traits include, irritability, muscle tension, and again, sleep disturbance (DSM-5, 2013). And although the anxiety may not reach the clinical level, many officers still may suffer impairment in both their social and professional interactions without ever identifying the root of the problem. One thing is for certain, a career in law enforcement is not going to get any easier, with ever-increasing political pressures. Unfortunately, the unforeseen victims are the cops and their families. As this book has illustrated, there are many psychological and physiological effects that take their toll on a police officer both in the short term and in the long term. Short term effects are lower performance, burnout and distress. The long term effects include various health problems, increased risk of disorders, divorce, interpersonal problems, and even death.

In the future, I hope law enforcement will come together and take more buy-in in their people. This can start by reexamining the shifts officers work and how just by changing the times, may be healthier. Other options would be limiting the hours worked and making mental health a priority rather than a silent killer.

I also think agencies can change the culture to realize it is acceptable to seek help and focus on self-care. The external factors are always going to be there, but it is up to the police culture to change and look within so as to limit the mental casualties suffered from the domestic war that is being fought daily.

Through psychoeducation, departments and individual officers alike can become more aware of the potential dangers that are happening inside their mind and body. It is no wonder why society and the media think we are indestructible, because we do too. The outsiders do not view us as human, but we have not given them any reason not to. If you recall part of self-mastery is being able to self-analyze and recognize our own strengths and weaknesses. Hopefully this book has provided the reader with a better base to build upon. After all, the other part of self-mastery is the constant sharpening of the one's knowledge and skills. The bar has been set high and those of us in the profession have to do it better than ever before. If you cannot afford to go back to school, take it upon yourself to self-educate. Read the suggested books I provide in the last portion of this book. Go out shooting, put yourself through some training classes, and get your hunting license. Have the mindset that you are a warrior and have a must larger duty on earth to fulfill than most. And lastly, exercise your brain as much as your body.

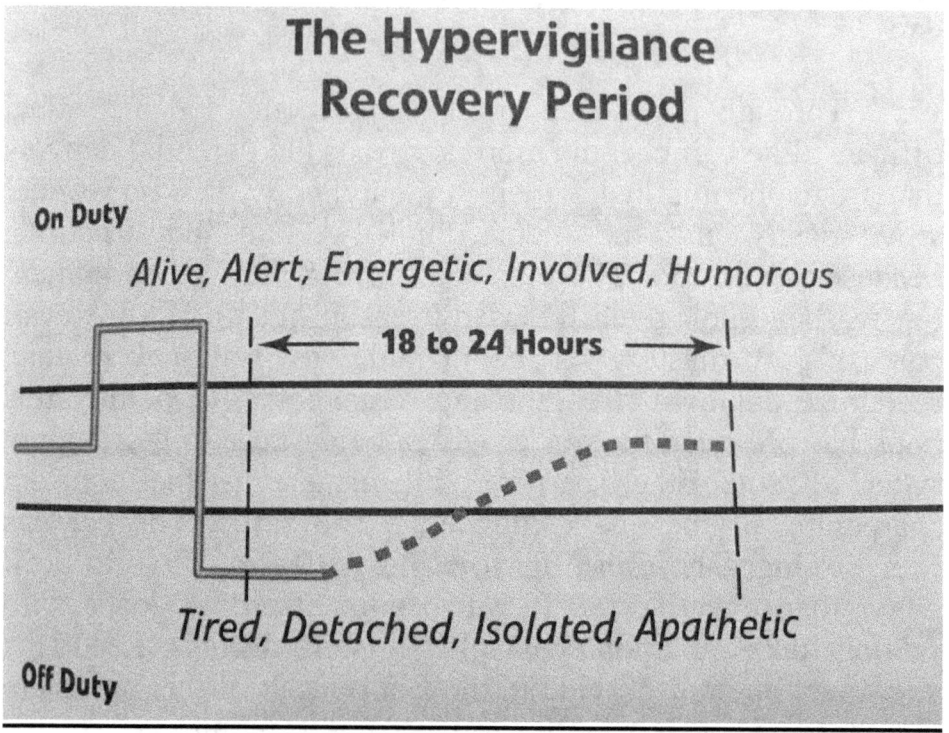

Dr. Gilmartin's hypervigilance rollercoaster

Chapter 6
WARRIOR VS. CRIMINAL JOURNALIST

"I am a soldier, I fight where I am told, and win where I fight."

-*Patton*

I have seen several articles on Facebook and other social media outlets debating the difference between the warrior and guardian police cultures. The fact that we even have to discuss such things disgusts me to no end, but I felt the need to note it in this chapter, for I believe the true message of this book is hopefully to illustrate the importance of *mindset*. Because regardless of what background or decision-making process one derives from, having the proper mindset is the backbone of this job. Frankly, we must have the mindset of a warrior to truly fulfill our calling. And I am not just talking about the cop on the beat, I am also speaking to the administrators, policy-makers, union reps and trainers/instructors out there. We must not lose the warrior mindset for we inevitably will see the amount of on-duty deaths continue to rise. I do not care if the word warrior is used to describe our mindset, honestly it does not matter what word we use; the outlook is the most important. I feel the word warrior will suffice for our purposes though, for all of the prior warrior cultures that came before us succeeded because of their *dominant aggression*. It was usually politics and logistics that was the fault of their demise, much like we have seen in the contemporary world of Law Enforcement.

Navy SEAL Mark Divine in his book, "Unbeatable Mind," fully embraces the warrior culture and points out that the warrior does not live in the past or the future.

However a true warrior must live in the present. Living in the present is vitally important from a performance psychology standpoint, but also from a philosophical view as well. And as difficult as it may be, part of being mentally tough is not letting past events and the angst of future struggles consume us. As Divine states, "Today's where you need to target your thoughts and energy. Today's where there's respect to earn, training to accomplish, and money to make (2015)." To me success cannot be defined by external attributes like promotion, rather success is internal self-mastery. This mastery of one's self, paves the road towards "why," and money, power and status become a mere bi-product of true success. The warrior must never stop sharpening the mind and body or else they will become dull and un-dangerous. Now I am not getting all macho meathead and saying we need to be all protein drinking, tiny-T wearing, running 20 miles a day kind of guys, but one parallel to the "warrior" culture we can all learn from, is *craftsmanship.*

In the book, "So Good They Can't Ignore You," the author turns the concept of "follow your passion," on its head. Rather than preaching that one's "why," can stem out of having passion for a job, Newport believes, by putting in the work first, one can develop more appreciation for what they do (2012). Now how many Millennials have that mindset? I for one used to buy into the passion mindset, however as I found it really does set us up for burnout. Moreover, some people may never truly find a passion, so where does this leave them? Newport goes on to say, "Passion comes after you put in the hard work to become excellent, not before. In other words, what you do for a living is much less important than how do you it (2012)." Read that over again, and respond on your own career. For me, I know I realized after all this time, I was building upon my passion, or as Newport calls it, "career capital."

All the training courses I paid for myself and traveled to, was not only a way of padding my resume, but I was sharpening my own warrior's edge. I was building up my experience and becoming an expert in my craft. Notice that word, craft. Much like the warriors of the past; that is all the concept of their existence boils down to, they were just experts in their field or craft. With that said, as professionals, think about how we can become craftsman of our trade. Sure we can become more proficient with our weapons. And yes we can all become better at talking to people. These are things that can aide in making us more professional. But in a broader sense, think about all those salty cops we have seen that are Retired On Duty (ROD). They lost the passion for chasing bad guys decades ago, but I think around the same time, they also stopped being craftsman. It is at this point in our careers that goal-setting and departmental culture can play a huge role. Just imagine how great our departments would be if everyone wanted to be the best they can be at their niche. And when they became bored of that niche, they found another one or did it differently. Furthermore, if they failed to keep up, the slugs would be culturally shun from the ranks (instead of getting promoted). I had my boost to become the best I could be when I lost a mentor and close family friend to an on-duty shooting. Following that incident, I swore to myself I was going to continually develop my skills as a force options instructor. My thought process was that I did not want to go through that again, and if I could train my guys to the best of my ability, then I can die knowing I did my job of keeping them safe.

In Sparta, warriors were raised from birth and the entire community revolved around their warrior culture. The young boys would be trained to be tough both mentally and physically. They spent hours learning the techniques and tools of their craft and solidified the future of their existence. These true warriors developed their intuitional intelligence, expanded their awareness and were one, mind, body and soul.

Sound familiar?

-The answer is no because we are far from that now. In this day and age, universities believe in such things as "toxic masculinity," where they frown on men being men. The women in our society are becoming more dominant, while the men are being castrated. If we look at any high school across America, it is no longer the young boys getting into fights at recess. Instead we have morphed into a society where the young girls are violently attacking each other. I think one of the causes for this is women no longer need men in their lives. Now that women can be CEO's of companies, raise a family without a man's income and run for the presidency- women are now the aggressors. They do not need the warriors, hunters and gatherers to go out into the wilderness because they now can fend for themselves. In our concrete jungle, the women run shit and the men just take it. Our nation's military now will flip the bill for a sex change operation, young boys no longer have to do physical education in school, and the divorce rate is at an all-time high. Oh and not to mention, law enforcement agencies across the states are demilitarizing our equipment as first responders and the courts are convicting cops for doing their job. So the only question we must ask ourselves is: Are we truly raising men to protect us when Russia, Korea or Mexico decide to take us over?

The Knights, who were somewhat more refined, possessed the common trait amongst all warriors, which is controlled aggression. Some argue the Knights were the first police officers because they wore badges as a "coat of arms."

The coat of arms identified the knight and his allegiance to justice, chivalry and his royal leaders. Moreover, the Knights were often sworn in to protect the weak and fight for the general welfare of all (2017). In fact, some of the staples of modern law enforcement stemmed out of Knighthood, such as the wearing of the badge over the heart. Knights would wear a similar metal badge over their heart to shield them from joust strikes, leaving their dominant hand to fight with. Also, because the badge was over the heart, the badge would remind them of their pledge. The concept of the Knight's place within society was they were the protectors of those who could not protect themselves and the safeguard of life and property. This noble cause is what many police officers and agencies have steered away from over time. They have forgotten that what we do is not meant for just anyone and there should be a sense of pride that comes along with being a protector of the Sheep.

In any warrior culture, the Sheep in a Sheepdog's clothing would have been easy to spot. Sadly now the lines are far too grey. If a coward was exposed on the front lines of any previous warrior culture, he was killed, often on the spot; for a coward was no different than the enemy they faced. In today's military and law enforcement ranks, there are far more cowards amongst us then we think. But no longer are the days of pushing out the weak, rather we hire more and administrators give atta-boys for cowardly behavior like not engaging. This is a dangerous mindset to have and is neither of a warrior or even of a guardian nature. In most agencies we have developed what I refer to as a "criminal journalist," mindset. Much like a news reporter, we respond to the scene of a crime like Sheep running towards feed, and then write a thorough report on what occurred. And administrators are quite alright with this because there is no use of force, no questionable camera footage or citizen's complaints.

Yes my dear friends, we are reactive servants; no different than a plumber or tow-truck driver. Thus, it is easier to dismiss us when something does not go according to plan. Agencies can kick us to the curb because we are just a number and society thinks death should be expected because we took that risk taking the job. Rather than looking at the loss of a Warrior as a great loss to all, most people shrug their shoulders and move on. Which is another common theme of our masculinity stripped society; most people simply want to live their lives in denial that there is the potential for violence out there. Instead of prepping for it like the Spartans, we would much rather live in a safe space cocoon that keeps the threat of evil at a very far distance.

Case in point, when I first became a cop, many of my non-cop friends were uneasy at the fact that I carried a gun everywhere I went. Many of them were hunters, so it was not the threat of having a loaded gun around, it was more realizing that there was a potential for harm, a potential that they could be faced with force or violence. They would rather party and have a good time without that looming over their heads. Perhaps this is much more healthy way to live, but these are also the type of Sheeple that only know to stampede when the shit hits the fan. And this is the exact point I would make when they asked why I needed to wear a gun. I would turn it back on them and ask them who they were going to come to if the threat of violence arose? Just because I was the cop meant I would be called upon to act, so I might as well have the tools of a cop. Much like the Knight, I am the warrior the weak inherently seek out when they are frightened.

But it is all too clear there are less and less warriors to turn to in society. Young boys do not grow up playing with toy guns or make believe samurai swords.

Kids are not taught to be tough after they fall down. Instead young people stare into their IPads and let someone else do the imagining for them.

I am not at all implying warriors need to be weapons experts. Rather, I believe the word warrior encompasses someone who stands up for what they believe - who is strong and does not cower in the face of danger. Perhaps the word warrior is over-used and has lost its true meaning. With that said, a warrior can be many things, but for our purposes a warrior needs to be strong. With his muscles yes, but the true strength lies between his ears. And such mental power starts way before the first day of the police academy. Building up our future men starts at home when they are young boys. Instead of limiting our kids by giving them all trophies, eliminating competition and bombarding them with technology, we must allow them to do what comes naturally to them, to be boys.

The Indian warrior culture would promote young boys to explore, hunt small game and make toy weapons out of sticks. This boosted their warrior spirit, built up their resistance to pain and improved their hand/eye coordination. Ironically, all of these traits are what are missing from our young recruits now. Developing the warrior way is not some magical thing, again it all starts with mindset. The warrior cultures of the past knew their preparedness and willingness to fight was paramount to their survival. We as a society and a police culture have gotten away from this mindset, but it is my opinion that we must not lose our nation's warriors or the great powerful United States will fall much like Rome did many years before.

And I am not at all implying we should be all ruthless killers who storm through neighborhoods with reckless abandon. Rather, we must become more like the samurai, disciplined and controlled- but can turn it on when the time comes.

The traditional samurai code of honor, discipline and morality known as bushido–or "the way of the warrior"–clearly mirrors traits that law enforcement warriors must practice daily, both on and off duty (2017). The word "samurai" roughly translates to "those who serve." (Another, more general word for a warrior is "bushi," from which bushido is derived; this word lacks the connotations of service to a master. (2017). Again, words like service in reference to those who serve is perfectly in line with the work we do. Moreover, as the samurai evolved, so did their responsibilities, to include: maintaining law and order. In fact, there are eight Bushido virtues that still apply to today: Rectitude or Justice, Courage, Benevolence or Mercy, Politeness, Honesty or Sincerity, Honor, Loyalty and Character or Self-Control (McKay, 2008). The warrior code was the basis to how they functioned within their warrior class and their ways were adopted by society because they realized the importance of such a force. On that note, one can clearly see how we have strayed far away from this concept and society seems to repulse any idea of law and order. But instead of the leaders in law enforcement giving into the crumpling of this structure, we must change from the inside.

No, we mustn't all become tactical warrior ninjas, but take note from the code of Bushido and adapt our own. The profession as a whole has lost the honor in doing what we do. At times, it seems we have lost our heading and no one really knows what we represent. Unlike the military, law enforcement has no true mission. This makes it difficult for

Officers to stay motivated day in and day out because there is no real cause to keep fighting for. Granted, we protect the sheep, but how? As with all of the warrior classes I mentioned previously, it all starts with a code. Too many cops feel they are fighting for a lost cause, so instead of letting society dictate who we are, perhaps it is time we begin to abide by our own code across the states. After all, do people really just want us to show up and take a report? No, they want us to catch the bad guy that victimized them. Even if they do not want prosecution or fail to cooperate with the DA, the fact is the bad guy goes to jail for committing a fucking crime. That is the code we live for and it should guide all of our decisions. In-turn, the cowards seeping into this profession will soon be found out because they will not fit such a mold. It takes a true warrior to want to have the desire to professionally hunt for evil, regardless of the risk of their personal safety. It takes a coward to drive slow and show up to take the report. Which one are you gonna be?

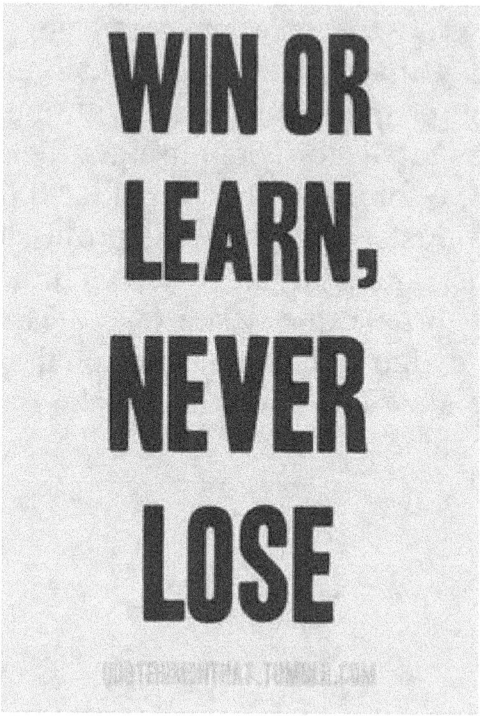
WIN OR
LEARN,
NEVER
LOSE

Chapter 7
LEADERSHIP

"No good decision was ever made in a swivel chair."
- Patton

I originally was not going to write a chapter on leadership, however after much thought I realized a discussion about leadership would be a great way to tie this whole book together. After all, if we cannot lead ourselves, how are we ever going to lead others? We are all leaders in one way or another. Whether it be the cop on the beat that the people turn to for leadership, or the Chief of Police (who ideally should be the best example of what a leader is). When the rookie officer looks at his/herself as being a leader within the community to which they work, a much more global sense of responsibility comes over them. The fact is most people are sheep and need someone to guide them. I can prove this by looking back at all the times I have been asked for advice or explained to parents how to raise their children while at work. If all else fails, call the cops, they solve problems!

But following the worst eight years of leadership this nation has ever seen, is that really what we want and need a leader to be? A manager puts out fires, a leader creates them. A good leader will create a fire in the people's hearts to be better. A great leader will create new leaders to take his place. The ultimate leader will unite people and provide them with something to strive for. To that end, there is a reason I quoted Patton at the beginning of each chapter. Not only was he a combat genius, but his leadership style very much mirrors mine. He was widely known as being arrogant and pompous, but such personality traits are almost needed in a leader. (Axelrod, 1999). Patton's drive and the way he carried himself was what made him such a one of kind character.

This uniqueness is also a trait that leaders must have because they cannot be predictable. Rather, great leaders must be reliable (1999). Frankly, much of what Patton represents is what most of our leaders in law enforcement are missing now a days. The quote below taken from the book, "Patton On Leadership," still rings true to our managers in the profession today:

"Does not make any difference what the rank is for promotion. Could be for a colonel or corporal. Picking the right leader is the most important task for every commander. When I have a promotion to make, I line up all of the candidates and give them a problem I want them to solve. I say 'Men, I want a trench dug behind a warehouse. Make this trench eight feet long, three feet wide, and six inches deep.' That's all I tell them. I use some warehouse that has windows or a large knot hole. While the candidates are checking out the tools they want to use, I get inside the building and watch through the window or knot hole. The men will drop all of the spades and picks on the ground behind the warehouse as I watch. After resting for several minutes, they will start talking about why I want such a shallow trench. They will argue that six inches is not deep enough for a gun placement. Others will argue that such a trench should be dug with power equipment. Others will say it is too hot or too cold to dig. If the men are officers there will be complaints that they should not be doing such lowly labor as digging a trench. Finally, one man will give an order to the others, 'Let's get this trench dug and get out of here. Doesn't make any difference what that old SOB wants to do with the trench.' ...That man get's the promotion. (1999).

I do not want to bore the reader with leadership do's and don'ts, but much like the rest of this book, it is important to get you thinking. Thinking about the leaders within our own agencies and how they are missing the ball. And more importantly, taking a look inside ourselves and how to lead both ourselves and others. As Patton pointed out we cannot keep promoting good test takers. I have illustrated before, part of what makes any good shooter, athlete, or performer is the ability to self-analyze. Perhaps even looking through the lens from the outside in, or even better from what is commonly referred to as a bird's eye view. This action allows us to step out of our own biases and paradigms to see what we can do better. Moreover, as peak performers we should be constantly looking to sharpen the edge of the sword anyway, and leadership is just another integral part of that equation.

Leadership starts with self-leadership. A leader cannot allow their own insecurities or agendas get in the way of their relationships. We have all fallen victim to those vindictive or egotistical types that clearly look out for #1 first and foremost. Even if they seemingly want to help subordinates, it is usually only to make themselves look better. Much like in the book, "The 7 Habits of Highly Effective People," we must always ask ourselves if decisions are a "win-win," for both parties involved (1988). Once we see things through this lens, we can see that supervisors are often just looking for their own win, but not necessarily a complete win for others. Leaders will always look out for what is best for their troops, even if it may mean they have to fall on the sword.

One of my favorite books on leadership, "Extreme Ownership," is entirely about this main concept. Jocko writes, "Extreme ownership. Leaders must own everything in their world. There is no one else to blame (2015)."

Now how many Sergeants do that on a daily basis? I am going to guess, not a lot. Some would blame this on their ego, however based on what I have seen, it is more because they are scared. As I have eluded to in previous chapters, many spineless actors have made it into supervisorial roles, and are insecure both in and out of work. Thus, they are far too insecure to man up and admit their faults. As a result, we get the supervisors that would rather throw down a write up versus stand up for their people. Because it is all about how it looks to the next guy up the chain. The preverbal shit truly does roll down hill.

This job is hard enough as it is and our so-called leaders are not making it any easier. Statistically officers do not commit suicide because of the shit they see on the street, rather it's the bullshit that happens inside the building that pushes them over the edge. But administrators forget about the human capitol they should be investing in. Instead, cops do what they have done their whole career. They do what they have been trained to do. When a street cop promotes, he hunts people. They put cases on people and document write-ups like a criminal history. But what is forgotten, is what this is really doing to the employee. Is this truly what is best for the organization? Discipline is intended to curb behavior or better train someone. Rather, administrators are more focused on the documentation trail that protects them from liability. I saw a very pro-active cop get messed with so much that he simply stopped being pro-active. On one occasion he responded to assist some of our Detectives that were calling for help in a neighboring jurisdiction. While en route there, they came on the radio and claimed the responding units could slow down. However, being like any other cop I know, the young officer "California stopped," some stop signs to still get there.

Normally he would have been okay, but he was driving the new fancy traffic unit that had a dash cam in it. So when they reviewed the Tasing that happened when he got there. Yes you read that right, he still had to use force when he got there because the Detectives were in-fact not okay. But anyway, on the footage, they watched him roll a few stop signs on his way. And even though the use of force was completely justified and within policy, they still decided to ram the driving down this guy's throat. When I heard of this, I actually went to that supervisor and reminded him the ultimate goal of a write up. As if he had never heard that before, he looked at me as if the light bulb had went on. I asked him if a write up is really going to get a cop to never roll through a stop sign again. But just like any other spine less administrator, he disagreed and still wrote the kid up. This is a prime example of not seeing the bigger picture; that bird's eye view of the ripple effects decisions like this have not only on that individual but also on the entire organization as well.

Another cancerous mindset I have seen in departments, is the "That's the way it's always been," mentality. I personally have heard this quote far too many times in my career and it is crippling to agencies. I believe one of the reasons for this attitude is un-educated people being promoted. Like I have stated before, I do not mean they do not have degrees because a degree does not make the man. But what I am referring to is the types of people that remain stagnant in their growth. They do not read articles, books or want to train their minds and bodies. They essentially repeat their first year of their job thirty times and retire. And yea they make Sergeant or Lieutenant but what have they really done in their careers? What legacy did they leave?

Instead of writing a conclusion to this book, this chapter on Leadership will provide the reader with both a summary of the past chapters and forethought to where we go from here. We are all leaders and we must take our profession by the horns. We really can be our own worst enemy and not to be cliché, but we have to be the best we can possibly be. This is includes hiring the right people, firing the wrong people and taking care of our people. I am obviously a huge proponent of training, but plain and simple, some people just aren't cut out for this job. We cannot just hire anyone with a pulse just to fill a position. I would rather be short-handed than to have some slug next to me and I feel most real cops feel the same way. To that end, we cannot continue to keep folks after an endless FTO period for fear of litigation or because we need to fill a spot. This is called negative retention and leaders must know when to cut ties. Because once these soup sandwiches get off probation, it is nearly impossible to get rid of them and we are stuck with them for a career.

Lastly, law enforcement leaders must stop castrating good employees. A servant leadership mentality must be developed and taking care of the good people we do have should be a priority. Part of this can be done by learning up on the psychological and physiological effects of use of force and human decision making under stress. In-turn, instead of looking at an incident through the eyes of a civilian, we can better care for our troops by better understanding them and why they do what they do.

Leadership is a mindset and supervisors should never ask their subordinates to do anything they would never do. We get paid to make decisions on our feet that could be potentially life or death. Leadership can play a vital role in which side the cop falls in that.

As I have illustrated previously, policies, procedures and politics only cloud the vision of the cop on the beat, thus slowing down their responses. Strict policies, frivolous write-ups and Monday morning quarter-backing can cause Officers to suffer from deathly mental noise. Instead of thinking through how to survive and come out a winner, they will be thinking how not to get into "trouble," with admin. As we have seen in this book, there are many influences that are at play in our minds, and the lack of support from admin should not be one of them. When Officers travel from the sub-conscious to the conscious and vice-versa, the number one thought should be to win, and how to go about doing that professionally. This is where leadership can have a vital role in cop decision-making.

From the moment we are born, we are looking for leadership. Frankly, most people throughout their adult lives need some sort of leadership, whether it be at work or in life. There have been countless books written on the topic of leadership and most of us have an idea of what a good leader is comprised of. However the unsung hero of many organizations is the "informal" leader. In the textbook, "Organizational Behavior, Human Behavior at Work," Newstrom defines an informal leader as a person who has the largest amount of status in the informal organization and emerges to exhibit influence on the informal group leaders (2011). Some would argue this is a form of power, but it should be noted the author did not mention authority.

Many so-called leaders are actually in a position of authority but fail to truly lead their subordinates because they lack influence. As in the article, "The Difference between a Leader and a Manager," author Rick Johnson simply states, "A leader must lead by example, whereas a manager uses direction and enforcement of policy and procedure to accomplish specific tasks, (Johnson, 2007)." Thus, the people look to the informal leader for guidance on their own organizational behavior.

On any school play yard, one can see the leaders amongst the groups and cliques that the majority seem to follow. The same can be said for most business organizations. Of course a person can develop leadership skills, however I would argue that most leaders have a natural ability to lead. It is unknown if people inherently are lazy, insecure or quiet, and that is why they tend to follow the leader. This "Social loafing," is defined as when an employee lessens their output when they think their contributions to a group cannot be measured (2011); Relative to the leader, who is respected, outspoken and confident. As a result, the majority of followers become content with allowing the leader to influence their thoughts and behaviors, and to be the spokesperson of the group. So one must continually ask themselves, Who are you? A leader or a follower?

The answer for this question for me comes relatively easily. For the majority of my life, I have been that playground leader, team captain of the sports team, and a force to be reckoned with at work. How I came to be this way I do not know, however the title of "natural leader," has been both a blessing and a curse. Having the respect of your peers is paramount so as to become an informal leader.

Because I do not cower to authority, teammates and co-workers have often gravitated towards me for leadership. However, the drawback to that was when coaches, teachers and managers recognized my influence on their subordinates as well. More often than not, I fell into a power struggle between the formal leadership and my peers. The formal leaders would be looking to use me to lead their people, however if I did not see eye to eye with them, conflict would quickly arise.

In an article actually written about the informal leadership amongst nurses titled, "Informal leaders and cultural change," the author notes an important aspect of being an informal leader; "Team members often address concerns and issues with the informal leaders that are not shared with managers (Krueger, 2013)." I suppose this is part of the reason I evolved into the role of informal leader amongst the patrol division because I not only voice my opinion openly, but also allow others to vent to me about concerns within the organization. Moreover, it is perhaps their hope that because of my position of leadership I will voice these concerns with the higher ups. This is where the mindset of the formal leaders comes into play. In my agency this feedback appears to be complaining to them, rather than being good leaders and assessing the opinions of their subordinates. Thus, I return to my role as informal sounding board to my peers and attempt to supply them with the best advice I see fit.

A new push in police work is "Procedural Justice (2015)." The concept is to take a more progressive approach to both citizen contact (external) and within law enforcement agencies (internal). Internally, agencies want to give the employees a voice and have more "transparency."

In the article "Explaining officer compliance: The importance of procedural justice and trust inside a police organization, (2015)." The authors touch on the "us vs. them," dynamic that is no longer just an external dilemma. Many employees now feel this way about their leadership, myself included. I recently attended a training course on this very topic and the instructors even opted to do separate courses for the supervisors and line-staff, further illustrating the wedge between us. I was later asked by an administrator, that because I am a leader within the organization, he needed me to buy-in to the concept of procedural justice for it to work amongst the troops. However, the informal leader inside me leans more towards using the pillars of procedural justice to use against the administrators when they do not abide by them.

All in all, the informal leaders can be both a blessing and a curse to any organization. I am a prime example of how information can be disseminated up, down and laterally with either a positive or negative spin. Much like my supervisor recognized, formal leadership can benefit from using their informal leaders as a positive information source. However, it is seldom that my views and values align with my administration, further cementing my role as a resource for the people. Hence, in one's career they often have to choose between many different roles and alliances, such as follower and leader or formal and informal leadership. But this cannot be determined by the organization, rather one must identify within themselves who they truly have always been, on the playground, on the field or in life.

An internet search of the definition of 'peak performance,' revealed it is, "a state in which the person performs to the maximum of their ability, characterized by subjective feelings of confidence, effortlessness and total concentration on the task (2015)." It should be also noted that other definitions within the search focused on the word 'peak,' and mentioned such words as summit or climax. Thus implying there is a down slide or performance less desired. Garfield in the book Peak Performers, however illustrates how a true peak performer is constantly overcoming adversity and ever-growing; in-turn, maintaining 'peak' performance. Achieving this is often easier as an individual, so how does one become a peak performer as a leader to others within in an organization? (1986). "Peak performers talented at course correction will fall in love with a mission, but not with their own ideas. They are adept at getting out of their own way (1986)."

To expand on that, a peak performer is one who has plasticity in their thoughts. In other words, they will not become so hell bent on the "that's the way we've always done it," mentality, but rather they will welcome new and better ways to do things. And because of that forward thinking, others will grasp onto such leaders. Instead, what is common in law enforcement is a 'position-style leader,' which is a leadership style in which the leaders influence others by virtue of their appointed or elected authority; most effective in a climate of instability (2013).

We can all think of supervisors like this that only have authority because of what is on their sleeve or collar, but they do not truly demand respect. A story that comes to mind for me is when a Sergeant of mine thought I was attempting to disobey his orders by not contacting a loiterer in front of a local 7-11. In a display of power, he yelled over the radio that he arrested the guy down the street and he wanted me to come to transport the dude. When I spoke to him later about the misunderstanding, he patted the stripes on his sleeve and said, "That's why you'll arrest him." Now I am sure many of us have experienced such egotistical non-sense, but one can only imagine how that eroded our relationship from that point forward. Insecure supervisors that play stunts like this, only do it because that is all they have. These are the same types that adhere to the letter of the law about policy and make decisions based on the fear of getting into "trouble." This is the complete opposite of a leader, who motivates their subordinates to do what is asked of them.

"Alignment occurs when individuals perceive that contributing to an organization produces direct contributions to their personal mission (1986)." Moreover, there is no true organizational mission when most of the employees are simply collecting a paycheck and going through the motions. As a leader, one must recognize the change within the organization and the people. "One consequence of that increasing awareness is a decreasing willingness to be mere cogs in a big wheel. Uniformity and conformity frequently do not elicit the most productive forms of team work (1986)." To that end, a true leader will not only listen to the troops but make changes to improve their environment. Plus, recognize them when they do a good job. This will improve overall job satisfaction that leads to be better performance (1986). As Garfield pointed out, "A leader is not an administrator who loves to run others, but someone who carries water for his people so they can get on with their job (1986)."But , there is a fine line between helping the troops and being a micro-manager. If there is no vertical trust, the entire system fails. "Without commitment and involvement at the top, there is no extraordinary effort from the ranks (1986)."

In essence, to truly be a peak performer leading others, one must first be a peak performer as an individual. Constantly learning, seeking out changes, having mental agility, recognizing and motivating your people, and creating future leaders (2013). With that said, not all peak performers are good leaders. Obviously many Chiefs have risen through the ranks for a reason, but perhaps have reached their maximum potential, or 'peak.' After all, a person can perform a task or position, but not necessarily at their peak. Law enforcement is in a very interesting time and our leadership will be vitally important in determining our future. I may sound like a broken record, but it is all about hiring, training and mindset. We have to hire the right people for the job. We have to train them to be warriors. And we have to lead them with the right mindset. The media and politics are putting cop's lives at risk and I do not see an end to that in sight. But instead of cowering to those who believe we are always wrong anyway, why doesn't our leadership stand for what is right?

As I have said many times throughout this book, my main goal of this book is to get the reader thinking- thinking about how we make decisions as both individuals and as an organization. Also, thinking about who we are hiring and what the make-up of law enforcement is going to be in 10, 20 and 50 years ahead. And lastly, thinking about who we are and how we can be better. Share this book with your co-workers, family and friends in an attempt to provide them with a sneak-peak on how true cops see the world. Perhaps then the mind behind our blue eyes will be a little less mysterious. In-turn, at least those in our inner circle can better understand what is abnormal to them that is all too normal for us.

We are slowly killing ourselves and the crooks are not the only ones to blame. The shit that happens on the carpet claims far more lives than the bad guy on the street. But the stress we put on our officers is a slow and sneaky killing process. It is time law enforcement leaders take a real long hard look internally and ask themselves if they truly want to live with that on their conscience in the sake of saving face with the media. Be a leader, not a follower. Run towards the fire fight. And most of all stay dangerous.

Chapter 8
Annotated Bibliography and Suggested Reading

1)   Page, J.W., Asken, M.J., Zwemer, C.F., & Guido, M. (2016). "Brief Mental Skills Training Improves Memory and Performance in High Stress Police Cadet Training." Society for Police and Criminal Psychology Journal, 31:122-126. Springer, Pennsylvania.

This peer-reviewed article is in-line with the main theme of my research. The Society for Police and Criminal Psychology Journal is highly respected in the field for up to date and pertinent information. In short, the authors found through empirical evidence how psychological performance training, such as breathing techniques, mental imagery and attentional focus, has reduced stress in police cadets. Which in-turn aids in cognitive processing, better memory recall, arousal control and greater overall confidence. Thus resulting in better decision-making, which is the ultimate goal of training. This experiment was relatively short, so the effects of a longer training period would clearly show even greater results, but this article illustrates the point of my research.

2)   Colin, L., Nieuwenhuys, A. Visser, A., & Oudejans, R.D. (2014). "Positive Effects of Imagery on Police Officers' Shooting Performance under Threat." Applied Cognitive Psychology 28: p. 115-121. Wiley Online Library.

Again this article explores the many benefits of mental skills training for police officers, but delves deeper in namely mental imagery. Although the authors are from the Netherlands, their research of Human Movement Sciences is still applicable to American Law Enforcement. The most important takeaway I took from the article was that mental imagery strengthens the neural pathways needed to perform the action in real life.

So much like my research, mental imagery can assist in quickly developing a trainee's intuitional decision-making because they have already done the action so many times in their mind's eye. Also another bi-product would be increased confidence and decreased anxiety, which is always a plus in any performance domain.

3)   Birrer, D. & Morgan, G. (2010). "Psychological skills training as a way to enhance an athlete's performance in high-intensity sports." Scandinavian Journal of Medicine and Science in Sports. Volume 20, p. 78-87. Wiley Online Library.

This article is important because it creates the nexus between the "high-risk," professions with high intensity sports, such as those that entail physical contact. The police athlete must battle injuries, recovery and self-assessment, just like a regular athlete so "Psychological Skills Training (PST)," can benefit those in police work as well. This article will tie in and expand on the other mental skills training articles but also expand on the athletic side of high risk professions.

4)   Nazam, F. & Husain, A. (2014). "Enhancing sports and exercise performance through cognitive interventions." Indian Journal of Positive Psychology, 5(1), 28-32. Indian Association of Health Research and Welfare.

Another peer-reviewed article that really illustrates a variety of "cognitive interventions." Even this verbiage is noteworthy because cognitive training assists the pre-cognitive decision-making process, which is the time frame this research is geared towards. And although this article is meant for those in sports, I believe it is totally relevant for the police athlete.

To that end, I hope my research can show the importance of transferring sport psychology techniques over to the high risk domain. Some techniques in this article are thought-stopping, relaxation techniques, mental toughness and positive self-talk. Essentially the points made in this article will pick up where the previous articles left off as it pertains to the police athlete and mental skills training.

5)   Arble, E., Lumley, M.A., Pole, N., Blessman, J., & Arnetz, B.B. (2017). "Refinement and Preliminary Testing of an Imagery-Based Program to Improve Coping and Performance and Prevent Trauma among Urban Police Officers." Journal of Police and Criminal Psychology, 32: 1-10. Springer, Detroit MI.

Again these authors address the many benefits to mental skills training for law enforcement officers, however they also reveal how mental imagery can prevent the maladaptive responses to stress and trauma. This self-care is another important, but forgotten, part of the performance of police officers. In essence, the message of this article is by conducting preventative mental skills coaching, officers are more likely to accept it, versus addressing a mental "problem," after the fact.

6)   Iaccino, J.F. (1993). "Left Brain-Right Brain Differences: Inquiries, Evidence, and New Approaches." Lawrence Erlbaum Associates, Publishers. New Jersey.

Although this book is somewhat outdated, it will serve as foundational research into the left-brain and right-brain argument. Obviously research has come a long way since the 1990's, however the simplification of the hemispheric tendencies will be beneficial when my research delves into analytical and intuitional decision-making.

After all, my inspiration for this research stemmed out of believing some of the police trainees were "right-brain" or "left-brain," dominant, but further research showed that we do have different decision-making styles, but more mid-brain and frontal orientated.

7)   Roskes, M., Sligte, D., Shalvi, S., & DeDreu, C. (2011). "The Right Side? Under Time Pressure, Approach Motivation Leads to Right-Oriented Bias." Association Psychological Science 22(11) 403-407. SAGE Publishing.

This peer-reviewed article researched soccer goalies and how they must make rapid decisions. The theory was that the goalies were biased towards using the right side of their brains when there is great time pressure, because the left hemisphere is more calibrated. The problem with the archival data they drew from is skewed because animals cannot produce cognitive thought like humans. Also much of the right brain and left brain research was conducted on humans without healthy brains so obviously the brains are not going to process information the same way. However, this article is still good to compare and contrast the different research out there.

8)   Newmark, T. (2012). "Cases in Visualization for Improved Athletic Performance." Healio.Com/ Psychiatry. Psychiatric Animals 42:10.

There has been research using FMRI's that supports a clear difference between the right and left hemispheres. During visualization, a shift in activity can be seen between the left and right hemispheres. According to this article, the right brain is associated with imagination while the left is more logical. Thus, the transfer from the logical to the creative enhances visual imagery and performance. Moreover, the right brain imagery makes the visualization more vivid.

So if the act is more clear, the more real the mental rehearsal. It should be noted, it is very difficult to hook an officer or soldier up to an FMRI in a real environment, so this is most likely the reason for a lack of research in the field.

9)   Kahneman, D. (2011). "Thinking Fast and Slow." Farrar, Straus and Giroux, New York.

This book is has become the staple of decision-making and the author is widely respected for his efforts. The main takeaway from the book is the author's illustration of the 'System 1,' and 'System 2,' systems in the brain. Basically System 1 functions with little or no effort and is more automatic; whereas System 2 is more like the complex analyzer of choice and concentration (2011). This book is great because it explores common decision-making as well as other domains, such as business. In-turn, the points of the book show the importance of the more global view of performance psychology, versus the limiting sport psychology lens.

10)   Gladwell, M. (2005). "blink, The Power of Thinking Without Thinking." Little, Brown and Company. New York.

This book was written by another popular author that presented yet another view on decision-making. The second part of the title truly explains the basis of my own research.
In order for police officers to "get out of their own way," they must learn to make more intuitional decisions. Actually like Gladwell points out, they must "thin-slice" information so as to make snap judgements, which are faster in a time crunch (2005). This book is a great break away from the hemispheric theories, and changes the focus more on information processing and intuition.

11)   Raab, M. & Laborde, S. (2011). "When to Blink and When to Think: Preference for Intuitive Decisions Results in Faster and Better Tactical Choices." Research Quarterly for Exercise and Sport, 82:1 p. 89-98. ProQuest Journal.

Even though the word "tactical," was chosen for this title, it was meant for a sport setting, but still applies to tactical decisions in law enforcement. This peer-reviewed article takes the theory of people having deliberate and intuitional decision-making preferences and actually provides a few different definitions from a management, psychology and sport lens. Much like I hypothesized, the article totally illustrates exactly why those who are more intuitional make faster decisions under time constraints. This is also the first time, we see the word "expertise," coincide with intuition. This topic will tie in nicely with the need for mental imagery so as to create maximum exposure to information processing, which is what separates the expert from the novice (2011).

12)   Rahman, M. (2009). "Understanding Naturalistic Decision Making Under Life Threatening Conditions." British Computer Society. London, UK.

Naturalistic Decision Making (NDM) is another framework of intuitional processing the fight or flight dynamic that law enforcement, firefighters and military personnel face during a deadly threat.This article delves into the sub-conscious and conscious reactions to a threat, including the emotional aspects such as fear. Moreover, there is even mention of yet another theory on hemispheric processing, which is bottom up cognition. Also, there is a point about the evolution of the human mind and how we still have the same bias towards survival. Lastly, the paper leaves the reader with the question if the body reacts to the felt emotions or the scary stimulus first. This article will serve as the nexus between natural, emotional and cognitive decision making as it pertains to tactical decision making.

13)   Klein, G. (1999). "Sources of Power, How People Make Decisions." Massachusetts Institute of Technology.

This book is filled with great points about decision making, and again suggests intuitional decision making is better when time is of the essence, high stakes, inadequate information, ill-defined goals, poorly defined procedures, stress, dynamic, and there is a need for team coordination (1999). One interesting take on how experts come to a decision was surprising. Klein found that the expert does not analyze all of his options, rather it is the novice that attempts to explore all their options before selecting a course of action. The expert makes the first selection that presents itself, even if it may not be the "best." But even Klein admits most of our decisions consist of both intuition and analyzation. This will pave the foundation for the speed versus accuracy debate found in other readings.

14)   Klein, G. (2003). "How to use your gut feelings to make better decisions at work, The Power of Intuition." A Currency book, published by DoubleDay. U.S.

The same author explores the benefits to intuition, and takes it a step further into decision making in the workplace. One interesting note is how he explains the problems that stem out of policies and procedures such as slowing down the decision making process. I have seen this first hand in law enforcement, and such delay is dangerous. The analytical types attempt to make sense of what is going on, and there is not always time for it. Also, Klein talks about how technology makes us less intuitional, which is a problem in the high risk domain. He also provides the reader with tips for becoming more intuitional.

15)   Gluck, A. (2007). "Damasio's Error and Descartes' Truth, an inquiry into epistemology, metaphysics and consciousness." Scranton and London University. University of Scranton Press. Chicago, IL.

This book is very heavy, mentally, however it delves deep into conscious thought and the aforementioned debate of emotional and physiological responses. Furthermore, Gluck illustrates that our perceptions may be 'colored' by our previous experiences (2007). Hence our focus and processing of stimuli may be influenced or primed subconsciously, thus making our intuitions that much more unique and special; "the sixth sense." The other topic Gluck discusses is the feedback loop between emotions and fight/flight. This will be compared and contrasted in other readings.

16)   Sukel, K. (2016). "The Art of Risk, The New Science of Courage, Caution, and Chance." National Geographic Society. Washington, DC.

Sukel provides the reader with updated and contemporary views in neuroscience and psychology. Clearly the topic of the flight or fight center in the brain (amygdala), and the front lobe are portions of the brain that are of interest to my research, which this book explores nicely. Moreover, those two portions suggest that within the 300 milliseconds it takes to react to a threat, we are not thinking with either our right or left hemispheres, rather our mid-brain is reacting and the fore-brain does the thinking. For the purpose of the research, this 300 milliseconds is the portion of time most in question. How do we develop trainees to be intuitional in this span of time? The author talks about past experiences, however trainees do not have such experience to draw from and many interactions on the street are novel.

17) LeDoux, J. (1996). "The Emotional Brain, The Mysterious Underpinnings of Emotional Life." Simon & Schuster Paperbacks, New York.

LeDoux addresses the neuroscience behind rapid decision making, including the right and left brain argument, however he also really delves into the emotional reactions involved in high stress decision making. I liked how he defined several common phrases within the field, such as "quick and dirty," decisions, as well as "chunking." This book will be good to explore the emotional side that causes actions to our emotional reactions, often subconsciously or pre-cognition.

18) Grossman, D. & Christensen, L.W. (2008). "On Combat, The Psychology and Physiology of Deadly Conflict in War and in Peace," Third Edition. Warrior Science Publications, US.

This book is a staple of most Law Enforcement trainers and it has been groundbreaking in revealing the mental side of conflict for cops and military personnel. Grossman speaks of the emotions involved in a deadly encounter, but also harps on the heart rates that cause motor programming to degrade. Thus, he is a huge proponent of stress inoculation training, which is also important in this research.

19) Sharps, M.J. (2013). "Processing Under Pressure. Stress, Memory, and Decision-Making in Law Enforcement." Looseleaf Law Publications, Inc. New York.

The title of this book says it all, but to expand, the main points to take away are how the author talks about how we as humans were hunters and gathers and how our minds evolved into what they are today. This is important because I feel with technology, our minds our becoming more analytical and less intuitional, which is still very important for our nation's warriors.

Sharps also provides examples from the past where Officers have errored in their decision-making.

20)   DeBecker, Gavin, Taylor, T., & Marquart, J. (2008). "Just 2 Seconds. Using Time and Space to Defeat Assassins and Other Adversaries." The Gavin de Becker Center for the Study and Reduction of Violence a not-for-profit foundation, Studio City, CA.

DeBecker is a famous writer and has wrote several well respected books within the field of decision making. Again this book's title explains so much, and somewhat in line with the 300 milliseconds explained prior, DeBecker illustrates how most deadly encounters are done in 2 seconds; Moment of Recognition and Moment of Commitment (2008). Essentially, he believes we can prevent or at least give us more time to react by creating space. But provides examples of multiple assassination attempts where space is not an option, so we must see a threat before they become a threat.

21)   Van Horne, P. & Riley, J.A. (2014). "Left of Bang. How the Marine Corps' Combat Hunter Program Can Save Your Life." Black Irish Entertainment LLC. New York, NY.

A book that took the concept of seeing a threat beforehand to the next level, Van Horne explains how to stay "left of bang."The bang being the gunshot or bomb exploding, by examining one's environment and noticing "kinesics," a soldier or police officer can get out of dodge or react faster. This concept ties in with my research in two major ways: the first being that recruits must be trained in these concepts, in depth. Secondly, it explains how patterns can better develop our minds to be more intuitional.

22)   Siddle, B.K. (2008). "Sharpening The Warrior's Edge. The Psychology & Science of Training." PPCT Research Publications, Belleville, IL.

I enjoyed how this book broke down the survival motor programs, reaction time, and stress management, all the components to peak performance. Out of all the aforementioned law enforcement/ military training books, this is one of the few that actually provides performance psychology techniques such as visualization and breathing techniques. In-turn, this book supplies the reader with a summary of heart rate, emotions, neuroscience and performance psychology combined- mirroring much of the purpose of this research.

23)   Heitz, R.P. & Schall, J.D. (2012). "Neural Mechanisms of Speed-Accuracy Tradeoff." Center for Integrative & Cognitive Neuroscience, Vanderbilt Vision Research Center, Department of Psychology, Vanderbilt University. Nashville, TN.

When we examine the difference between so-called left brain and right brain thinking or analytical and intuitional decision making, essentially there is a tradeoff between speed and accuracy. On one hand, pre-cognitive reactions are faster, but not always the "best," option; whereas cognitive decisions are slower, but most obvious options are analyzed and concluded. The question we are left is which is "better," for law enforcement? Speed or Accuracy?

24)   Johnsen, B.H., Espevik, R., Saus, E.R., Sanden, S., & Olsen, O.K. (2016). "Note on a Training Program for Brief Decision Making for Frontline Police Officers." Journal for Society of Police and Criminal Psychology. 31:182-188. Springer.

An eye opening article that shows the importance of mental skills and situational awareness training in law enforcement. Perhaps Norway is ahead of the times, but the researchers correctly point out that traditional police training consists of physical skills and cognitive education, but rarely combines both or involves the feedback from the trainee. This further illustrates my call for psychoeducation becoming a more common practice in American Law Enforcement training.

25) Anderson, J.P. & Gustafsberg, H. (2016). "A Training Method to Improve Police Use of Force Decision Making." SAGE Open Vol 6. Number 2.

This article suggests something that may be good in theory but I am not sure it would work in reality due to the 'bravado,' nature of police work. The training method suggests a performance resilience and efficiency program that would entail officers attend regular sessions with a mental coach much like an athlete. The study saw positive results, and I think any mental imaging and breathing control would surely benefit any officer both on and off duty.

26) MacDonald, H. (2016). "The War on Cops. How the New Attack on Law and Order Makes Everyone Less Safe." Encounter Books, New York.

MacDonald went head first at the elephant in the room and discusses how the cops of our nation have become the enemy. Thus, officers need to be better and faster than ever before. With the attacks on cops on the street, in their own departments, in the media and in the courts, training is imperative. In such an unsteady time, some would argue cops need to be more analytical in their decision making, but I would argue the opposite.

It is obvious that no matter what officers do, they are always going to be wrong, so they might as well go home at the end of their shift. With that said, it has been proven intuitional decision making is faster, so Officers must develop their "6th sense," so as to rapidly react to a threat; versus exploring all of their options, fearing political judgement and getting killed.

Aamodt, M. (2013). Industrial/organizational psychology: An applied approach (7th ed.). Belmont, CA: Thomson-Belmont Wadsworth.

Garfield, C. (1986). Peak performers: The new heroes of American business. New York: W. Morrow (2015)http://medical-dictionary.thefreedictionary.com/Peak+Performance

Haas, N.E., Craen, M.V., Skogan, W.G., & Fleitas, D.M. (2015). "Explaining officer compliance: The importance of procedural justice and trust inside a police organization." Criminology & Criminal Justice. SAGE Publications.

Johnson, R. (2007). "The difference Between a Leader and a Manager." American Fastener Journal. ProQuest.

Kruegar, D.L. (2013). "Informal leaders and cultural change." American Nurse Today, 8.8. Healthcom Media.

Newstrom, J.W. (2011). "Organizational Behavior, Human Behavior at Work." McGraw Hill Education. New York, NY.